# *More* Secrets Of SUCCESSFUL Exhibiting

## Strategies, Tips & Insights

To Make Your Exhibiting
Dollar Work Smarter & Harder

From

Some Of America's
Leading Professionals

Susan Friedmann • Charles Greene III • John Hasbrouck
Sam Lippman • Jim Obermeyer • Mark S. A. Smith
Skip Cox • Christine A. Ellis • Elaine Cohen
Marcia A. Smith • Barbara Axelson

Compiled by

**Susan A. Friedmann**

Copyright © MCMXCVIII

Edited by: Valerie A. M. Demetros, Desert Jade Press,
Scottsdale, AZ

Cover Design and Page Layout by:  Ad Graphics, Tulsa, OK

Printed in the United States of America

Library of Congress Catalog Number  98-072841

ISBN 1-890427-05-5

Published by:

AVIVA
PUBLISHING

a subsidiary of Diadem Communications
P. O. Box 1850
Lake Placid, NY  12946-5850
(518) 523-1320


Additional copies of
*More Secrets of Successful Exhibiting*
can be obtained from any of the authors by calling
their individual number as listed with their chapter.


Quantity discounts are available.

# CONTENTS

# FOREWORD

If knowledge is power, then this is a powerful book. The knowledge contained in this second book of the Successful Exhibiting series comes directly from the experiences of prominent experts in the exposition industry. As you will learn, exhibiting is considerably more than simply booking space and ordering a booth – although that is often the extent of time and effort that some exhibitors invest.

The authors who have contributed to this worthy publication realistically cover a wide variety of topical issues by discussing areas vital to the success of an exhibit program, including how to justify your exhibit activities (and expenses) to management, how to benefit from public relations, how to market your show participation, program planning essentials, partnering with show management, determining what eye-catching activities will transpire in the booth during the show to increase traffic, and many other crucial factors.

Two essential areas that often fall by the wayside are measurement and the follow up of leads, so pay particular attention to these chapters. Accurate and credible measurement allows you to see if you are on the right course and cycles back to help you justify your exhibit program. Following leads is critical to your success. You cannot evaluate the success of your exhibit program solely by what occurs on the show floor. The sales that are made subsequent to the initial show floor contact should be distinguished as show leads for designation purposes.

Add a timely and important chapter regarding the special challenges of catering to the increasing volume of international clients, and you have a neat package of helpful and useful information that you will refer to over and over again.

Whether you are a seasoned trade show veteran or a recent college graduate, there is value for you within the pages of this book. Formal education is relatively new in this dynamic field. Publications such as this contribute greatly to the common body of knowledge that is so important for the increasing professionalism within the industry itself.

### *Patti J. Shock*

*Associate Professor and Department Chair Tourism and Convention Administration Department Harrah College of Hotel Administration University of Nevada, Las Vegas*

# INTRODUCTION

You asked for it and here it is, the second book in the Secrets series. Each piece of advice is gold dust. The nuggets of wisdom from our industry experts are precious gems that will add sparkle and richness to your exhibiting program. The more you dig, the greater the treasure you will find. If you want a fresh approach to exhibiting, if you want to excel and outshine your competition, then start reading now.

Discover eleven specialized chapters, jam-packed with cost-cutting, time-saving, results-producing techniques to increase your exhibiting success. Explore this gold mine of timely, practical, powerful information designed specifically for today's savvy exhibitor - whether you are a novice or well-seasoned veteran.

Once again we invited industry experts to share their knowledge, expertise and secrets, so you can tap into a vein of new and exciting opportunities to take your exhibiting program to a whole new level.

On a personal note, I am extremely grateful to my colleagues who are so willing to share their expertise. I appreciate their support, wisdom, and friendship in helping to raise the level of exhibitors' professionalism. Providing education is a crucial component to success.

Our words. Your actions. Your mining expedition.

*Susan A. Friedmann*

*The Tradeshow Coach*
*Lake Placid, NY*

# Speeding to Market Successfully

by
Christine A. Ellis

# Speeding to Market Successfully

Christine A. Ellis

*"We're late, we're late for a very important date."*

If there is one thing common to the entire international tradeshow industry, it's that everything, without exception, is time sensitive. The date for that very important tradeshow just isn't going to move. It is fixed. Nothing short of a catastrophe is going to change those plans. It will loom larger and larger as the date approaches – until that feeling of utter panic finally sets in as you and your suppliers skip meals, lose sleep and work around the clock in overdrive.

The result? Well, maybe not that bad, considering you had so little time to get everything done. The sales team didn't really complain – as far as you know, and yes, you did get some press coverage, and the booth looked fine and well, everyone liked the giveaways. But wait a moment. Could things have been different? Did you by any slight chance set any marketing goals? Did you have a promotional plan? Did you organize any pre-show marketing? Did you get any professional help? With hindsight and more time, could the show have been more successful?

Before you decide to race ahead like the hapless hare, take a tip from the wise tortoise and make a conscious decision to give yourself plenty of time. Whether you plan to exhibit for the first time or the tenth time, banish all thoughts of doing anything on a just-in-time basis. While this practice may be a splendid tool for organizing automotive production inventory, it will only cause you considerable grief as errors loom large and the cost of your tradeshow escalates.

To speed to market successfully, always take the following five steps:

- Pre-Show Planning

- Program Management

- Pre-Show Marketing

- Show-Site Management

- Post-Show Follow-Up

## Pre-Show Planning

Walk the show you plan to attend and imagine you are a prospective buyer. What catches your attention and why? Is it a booth's location, or is there a new, interesting or informative attraction? Survey the competition. Do they have any new technology, product displays, graphics, brochures or marketing themes? Ask yourself why some booths are crowded and some are empty? Notice that buyers and media people are often in a hurry and seem focused – usually following a list of pre-arranged appointments around the show.

> *"To market, to market, to buy a fat pig.*
> *Home again, home again, jiggety jig."*

Use the time to learn and experience new tradeshow techniques. Talk to people. Find out what a cross section of exhibitors and visitors think of the show. Are attendance figures going up or down? What is the ratio of large to small booths? Are there more or fewer outside events organized? Make some notes and if permitted, take photographs. Immediately following the show, request feedback from the sales team and your suppliers.

*"Three blind mice, three blind mice. Did you ever see
such a thing in your life as three blind mice?"*

If you are lucky, your target tradeshow will already have been integrated into your company's overall strategic sales and marketing plan. You will have clearly defined goals to reach and you must merely execute the plan and turn the tradeshow opportunity into a dynamic reality. However, as we all know, strategic sales and marketing plans are few and far between. It is more likely that there has not been even a hint of strategic thinking and you are running blindly ahead – skidding on the fast track toward the show. Start by calling on your sales colleagues to collaborate on a list of general show goals and objectives. Consult your notes and photographs from your show research and share the information with your team. Once your list of goals is agreed upon, specify and quantify the goals. Make sure all goals and objectives are realistic and achievable.

## Show Goals (Examples)

- **Launch new ABC product** – key task: design new product demonstration and graphics for booth

- **Test market new XYZ product** – key tasks: distribute samples of the product – design new graphics

- **Generate 20 new sales leads per day of the show** – key task: organize sales lead management

- **Improve relationship with top five customers** – key task: arrange meetings during the show

- **Support your industry** – key task: participate in one major association function during the show

## Program Management

> *"It just shows what can be done by*
> *taking a little trouble," said Eeyore.*
> *"Brains first and then hard work.*
> *That's the way to build a house."*
>
> – AA Milne – The House at Pooh Corner

Now comes the part where you need to set some time aside to do serious thinking. You will need to translate your goals into a specific action plan. What are you going to do on the booth? What are you going to show? What about the booth and the graphics – what about the theme?

At this point you should call in some experienced support – an exhibit house, tradeshow marketing company or tradeshow consultant. After all, the show should still be 9 to 12 months away and you have plenty of time. Provide your support team with a show brief or specifications: even if you are not working with an outside contractor, document your show data and goals – it will keep you on track.

- **Show Goals** – List and quantify your goals

- **Show Budget** – Imagine you are at an auction – set a limit for the show

- **Show Data** – Size of booth, dates of show, copy of the show manual, show profile, description of target audience

- **Facts** – Specific information, sizes and weights of your products, displays and demonstrations, corporate identity or logo requirements, PMS colors

- **Needs** – Meeting areas, hospitality, staff

- **Ideas** – Your suggestions on how the show goals can be achieved through the booth design

## Pre-Show Marketing

*"Simple Simon met a pieman, going to the fayre.*
*Said Simple Simon, to the pieman,*
*'Let me taste your wares.'"*

While it would be wonderful to bump into all those new prospective clients at the 'fayre,' it is highly unlikely. Pre-show marketing is fundamental to organizing a successful show. Exhibitor research[1] has proven that exhibitors who use promotions and take an integrated approach to their marketing attract up to 50% more visitors than those companies who do not. In other words, consider developing a simple key message or central theme, slogan or memorable graphic to create visual continuity and build recognition. Your theme, slogan or graphic should reflect your show goals and appear on all your marketing materials, including your pre-show mailer, advertising, press releases, show literature and on the booth itself. Some successful show themes include:

- [2] Talking Technology

- [3] Open to the Future

- [4] Shades of Blue

- [5] Solutions

---

[1] Source CEIR – Center for Exhibition Industry Research

With thanks and acknowledgment to the following, for use of their tradeshow themes:

[2] Andrew Smart – General Manger – Perkins Technology Inc.
[3] Bob Sampson – Exhibit Marketing Manager, MARCOM – Siemens Energy and Automation
[4] Tom Schoeneberger – Vice President – Blue Water Visual Systems Inc.
[5] Dr. Sergio Sedas – Business Development Director – Techmatec S.A. de C.V

## Show-Site Management

> *"Jack be nimble, Jack be quick,*
> *Jack jump over the candlestick."*

This is where all the time you have spent getting organized and planning ahead is going to really pay off. Your contractor is busy taking care of your booth and graphics, your on-site services are ordered, you have taken care of travel arrangements, hospitality events, pre-show mailers and you have everything under control. Or do you? Remember that anything can and will happen at a tradeshow. You have only a couple of days to stage a major event and even with the best will and time management in the world, things can go wrong that are entirely out of your control. Your booth properties could be stuck in customs at the border. Your product demonstrator could get ill. The booth might get flooded (this actually happened to someone – twice!). Keep a cool head and remember that shows always open on time and that there are ways to solve those last-minute headaches. Add these tips to your survival kit:

- **Arrive early**, even if you only have a pop-up booth that takes one hour to set up. You will probably still need carpet, an electrical service, lead retrieval, graphics, and show information. If you think you need just one hour, think again.

- **Be prepared**. Always aim to have the booth completed 24 hours before the show opens. Your show contractor will ruefully assure you with a wry smile that this is not possible. However, you should always try and allow a buffer of time to accommodate any unforeseen events and prevent you from running into expensive overtime with show contractors.

- **Stay calm**. No matter what happens, like *Dorothy in The Wizard of Oz, "hold on tight and don't lose your head."* Treat everyone with respect and issue clear, firm instructions. Appear cool, calm and organized and you will easily win the respect and help of the tradeshow contractors. Remember, you may need to return to the same convention site and deal with same contractors next year.

- **Be organized**. While your booth is being cleaned and polished by your contractors, organize the sales literature and giveaways and deal with those last minute panics of forgotten badges and parking passes. If you are super organized, take publicity photos of the booth, walk the hall, survey the competition and even find time to rearrange the plants.

## Post-Show Follow-Up

*"Peas porridge hot, peas porridge cold.*
*Peas porridge in the pot nine days old."*

Leads from tradeshows are always very hot. However, just like porridge or oatmeal, the longer they are left – the cooler they get. Pre-plan how you will handle all those tradeshow leads well before the show starts. Remember that you will arrive back from the show to a barrage of work, mail, faxes, e-mail and phone messages. Pre-planning will enable you to expedite those tradeshow leads quickly and professionally with the minimum of effort. The easiest method is to delegate the entire process to a lead-management company, or alternatively to a reliable colleague in the sales department.

Failing this, plan to prepare all your sales letters and follow-up correspondence at least three weeks prior to the show. Automate the process and make use of the show sales lead-retrieval database system. Talk to the show vendors about how you can make the most of their services.

## The Finish Line

When the finish line is in sight and you have shipped the last crate, paid the last supplier invoice and followed up on all the sales leads, remember that there is always room for improvement. Organize a post-show meeting with your sales group and suppliers. Ask for everyone's opinion and document the results. Do this while you still have everything fresh in your mind. Look back at your show goals and measure your results. Like Eeyore, you just might be surprised at what you can accomplish with a little extra time and trouble.

# Christine A. Ellis

Christine's career in international marketing spans three continents and a broad range of experience in business planning, strategic marketing, public relations and tradeshow marketing. Educated in England and a graduate in European languages, international marketing and economics,  Christine is an honors graduate of the Institute of Export and Professional Member of the American Marketing Association.

Christine has worked throughout Europe and in South Africa, rising to International Marketing Executive with a multi-national Engineering Group. In 1987, she relocated to Detroit and founded The Facet Company – a full-service marketing communications firm. Today, Christine is responsible for spearheading the four major brand areas of the company (technical marketing, collateral materials, tradeshow marketing and multimedia development) and for developing international business relations in Europe and Mexico.

# Facet

*"Some men see things as they are, and say, 'Why?' I dream of things that never were, And say, 'Why not?'"*
— George Bernard Shaw

Facet is a new media company specializing in international marketing communications and tradeshow marketing. Staffed by high-caliber European and American designers, engineers, marketing consultants and projects coordinators — Facet develops innovative solutions to complex marketing assignments for corporate, industrial and international clients. Facet is also an authorized distributor for Profilex custom modular display systems for EDI of Canada and Classic Displays Portable Systems. In 1998, Facet was presented with an award from the British Consul for outstanding service and support given to British exhibitors at the Detroit SAE'98 Show. Facet clients have received "Best in Show" honors from Michigan to Mexico City.

Facet is constantly improving its technology, knowledge and skill base, offering expert design in multimedia presentations, 3D animation and web-site development. At its facilities in Michigan, Facet regularly hosts functions for clients and invites speakers to present topics of interest from tradeshow marketing to video conferencing. Facet's operating philosophy and vision is based on a simple, 10-page Charter that focuses on its evolution, communication, integrity, quality and customer care.

For more information, contact:

The Facet Company
14940 Cleat Street
Plymouth, Michigan 48170-6053, USA
Tel: +(1) 734.453.3500
Fax: +(1) 734.453.3843
cellis@facetcompany.com

# How to Justify Tradeshows to Management

by
Mark S. A. Smith

# How to Justify Tradeshows to Management

## Mark S. A. Smith

You know that attending an upcoming tradeshow is right for your company. You've talked to some of your best customers and they'll be there. You've heard through the grapevine that your toughest competitors will be there. Your sales force has asked if you'll be exhibiting. And still the boss says, "No."

How do you justify tradeshows to management? How do you help them understand that the right tradeshow, done correctly, can take the company to new levels of success?

## What Holds Them Back?

When many managers think about tradeshows, they remember standing around all day handing out trinkets or getting drunk and throwing people in the pool. You know that those days are gone.

### Bad Past Experience

Find out if past experiences are blocking their decision. Ask the following:

- What has been your experience in the past with tradeshows?

- What is it about tradeshows that you think won't work for our company?

- What do you think might have to change for us to be successful at a show now?

- What would you need to know to feel comfortable with us going to a show?

### Colleague's Bad Experience

While asking questions, you may find that their reluctance to exhibit is based on the past bad experience of a colleague. You might ask, "What do you think it is that they did or didn't do that kept them from being successful?" Or, "What do you think has changed since then?" Challenge them with, "How do you know that we wouldn't be successful this time?"

### Funding

Perhaps what holds them back is a lack of funding for the show. If your company is like many, you have an advertising budget. Perhaps reallocating a portion of the ad budget to a tradeshow would be acceptable. To get their acceptance, you need to show your manager that the tradeshow expenditure will do better than the advertisements. Instead of focusing on the number of leads that the ads bring in, look at the number of sales closed from the leads brought in by the ad. Traditionally, tradeshow contacts lead to sales much more rapidly than any other marketing method, besides direct sales.

You may be able to show your manager that a request for tradeshow funding is worthwhile. Do this by creating a proposal outlining the costs and the return on investment.

### Reliance on Other Marketing

Perhaps your manager feels that the company has committed to plenty of other marketing programs and that tradeshows just aren't necessary. If this is the case, consider showing your manager **Figure 1,** *How tradeshows fit into the marketing mix.* Personal selling requires a live human involved in the sales process, whereas non-personal selling can be done with paper or electronic means such as audiotape, video, or WWW. Product description is where a prospect has the product described to them, and product inspection is where the prospect can touch, hold, smell, taste, see, stand on and otherwise inspect what you're selling.

Tradeshows cover all of the ways to communicate your message to a prospect. Your preshow promotion and exhibit offers product description and non-personal selling. Your exhibit staff and demonstrations allow personal selling and product inspection. And you can do this for hundreds and thousands of prequalified prospects at a properly selected tradeshow.

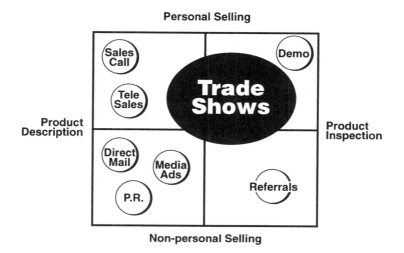

Figure 1: *How tradeshows fit into the marketing mix*

*No experience*

Perhaps your manager hasn't had any experience in tradeshow selling. Maybe they've come from an industry that didn't rely on tradeshows or was formerly in a position where they weren't exposed to tradeshows. In this case, you may wish to give a short presentation on the advantages of tradeshows in your market. Use the ideas in this book to create a compelling presentation that convinces them that a tradeshow, done properly, will work.

## What Management Wants to See and Hear

Knowing how to sell the idea of the tradeshow to your manager is a big part of your job. Knowing what words to use and how to make the presentation is important. Here are some ideas that can help:

*Show the Big Picture*

Most managers want to see the big picture. They need to know how tradeshows allow them do what they're hired to do. They don't need to see the specific details of exactly how the show will be executed, at least not in the beginning.

*What's a Customer Worth?*

Most managers understand that customers are worth a lot of money over the long haul. Savvy companies know that selling to existing customers is five to 10 times more profitable than finding a new customer. Tradeshows are a great way to keep existing customers.

Calculate what a customer is worth by multiplying your customers' average sales, with the average number of times they buy from you in a year and the average number of years they buy from you. This resulting figure is the average lifetime value of your customer. Is it worth going to a tradeshow to find more customers?

## *How are They Motivated?*

When making your tradeshow proposal, zero in on what motivates your manager. Focus on creating results more quickly and at a reasonable cost.

Listen carefully to how your manager talks about the business. If they want the business to grow, then tell your story about the tradeshow enabling them to hit their goal more quickly and more efficiently. If they talk about business survival, tell them that the tradeshow will keep the company alive because you'll keep the old business that your competition may get if you don't attend the show. And besides, what will the market place think if you don't attend the show?

## *Illustrate Success*

Managers need to have a level of certainty that the plan will succeed. If you have friendly competition – companies that call on your customers, but you don't compete head-to-head – interview them about their success at the tradeshow. Find out what new business they get and what old business they retain because of their participation. Present these as case studies of tradeshow success in your industry.

You can also increase your manager's confidence by including an appendix of checklists and budget items that he can review. Include a follow-up action plan that enlists the sales force. Let your manager know that your team is ready to act on the opportunity, guaranteeing success.

*Give Them Options*

Many managers need to choose from an array of options. Offer them a series of participation options, ranging from just going to the show and hanging out at the cocktail parties, to putting together a small, simple exhibit with two people, to creating a large complex exhibit. Give them price versus payback options.

## What Do You Want?

Understanding why you want to go to the show and what you want to get out of it can help you justify the show. Here are a few reasons that savvy companies use to make shows pay off.

### *Top 15 Reasons to Exhibit at Tradeshows*

1.  *Sell what you offer to visitors.* Without a doubt, this is the best reason to go to a tradeshow – not the only reason, but by far the best. Only 9%, on average, of attendees who visit an exhibit have been called on by a salesperson within the 12 months prior to a show. This means that more than 90% of the visitors will see you for the first time this year.

2.  *Sell what you offer to other exhibitors.* A reverse show, or one where you're targeting the other exhibitors, instead of the visitors, can work very well. Supply goods and services that the exhibitors use in their daily business, or could sell to their customers. You don't need an exhibit to do this. Just walk the show floor and collect business cards. Sell after the show is over: "You gave me your card at the show, could I have a few moments to speak with you?"

3.  *Get leads for your sales force to follow up.* Eighty-six percent of exhibitors go to shows to get leads and only leads. This is a good secondary reason to be at the show, but it should never be your number-one reason. When you gather leads, make sure that contests or drawings attract only people who can do business with you. Here's the acid test: If your sales people want your giveaway, it's a bad giveaway.

4.  *Network and trouble-shoot with other professionals.* You can share your war stories with others who have faced the same challenges and learn from more experienced pros in the business. Many companies walk away from the show with new insights on current challenges.

5.  *Establish industry positioning.* A show is a great place to announce to the world that you're a player. The more floor space you have, the bigger the player. You can fill space with plants, rented furniture, and sales people to make a major statement without spending lots of money on an exhibit.

6.  *Meet with existing customers.* You can make weeks' and months' worth of sales calls to your existing customers in a short period of time. Invite them to see what's new and offer them a special VIP gift.

7.  *Visit with people who are otherwise hard to meet.* At tradeshows you can get to key buyers who are otherwise unapproachable. Find out which shows your hard-to-see prospects attend, and have all hands watching for them.

8.  *Introduce new products to the market.* This works great if you can coordinate a product launch with

a tradeshow. Invite customers and prospects to come see your new offering.

9.  *Do market research.* In just a few days, you can try new offers out on thousands of buyers and fine-tune your pricing and product focus. Just change the signs on your exhibit to test different headlines and offers.

10. *Find new dealers, representatives, and distributors.* If you're looking for help distributing what you sell, put a small sign in your exhibit that stating *Dealers Wanted* or *Agents Wanted.*

11. *Find new employees.* It's virtually inevitable that job seekers will be walking the show floor. Put up a small sign: *Now Accepting Selected Applications.* Be discreet; you'll probably be contacted after the show, too.

12. *Conduct business meetings.* You can meet with business partners and prospective partners in just a few days. To do the same thing without the show would cost you thousands of dollars and weeks on the road. Many companies combine sales meetings with tradeshow events.

13. *Scope out the competition.* You'll get a clear picture of your competition's marketing strategy and a glimpse at their directions at a tradeshow.

14. *Get smart.* The educational sessions are good reason to go to an industry or association conference. If possible, be part of a panel or better yet, be a featured speaker at the educational program. Invite customers and prospects to see the program.

15. *Get media exposure.* The trade press are at industry and association shows. National media are at large consumer shows.

Let your manager know that your strategy is to pick several of these reasons and concentrate every bit of your effort on hitting the mark.

## Measure Outcome

Good management never argues with success. (If you're arguing that you don't have good management, change jobs.) So show your manager your success and you'll go to all of the tradeshows you wish.

### *Before the Show Starts*

You can predict tradeshow outcome by looking at the attendee list for this year or last year. Reviewing the titles of the people you do business with, what percentage of those people are at the show? If you have less than 15% coverage of your target market, choose another show.

Who exhibited at last year's show? If the bulk of your competitors attended, you'll probably want to be there. If one or two are there, you may wish to scope out the show before making the investment. Talk to friendly competition about their participation at the show. You can get some of the best information about a show's performance from them.

Talk to key prospects. Ask them if they plan to attend the show. Ask customers if they'll be going. If you get a high percentage of positive responses, you'll have a good show.

### *At the Show*

Many shows color code badges. If you can determine the color code for your prospects, count how many of these people are walking by your exhibit. Get a small hand-held counter like the ones used by ticket takers. Don't worry about missing a few people, you're looking for an overview of how many prospects are walking the aisles. If you're not getting your fair share, you may wish to change your signs and graphics on the spot. Or ask your sales people to be more aggressive in questioning visitors strolling by.

Ask visitors if they're getting what they need out of the show. Ask them if they think they'll attend next year. The answers to these questions will give you the best indication of the show's quality.

Quality control your leads to make sure that you're getting the information you need and that the people to whom you want to sell are stopping. Report the results of your on-the-spot survey to your manager.

*After the Show*

Require that all exhibit staff submit a single-page report on the show. Ask them to write their opinion of the show:

- Was it worthwhile?

- What did you do well?

- What should you do differently next time?

- What are the competitive trends?

- What are the industry trends?

These reports give you a good indication of the success of the show.

Also track sales from the show. Compare the list of customers after the show to the list of leads collected at the show. It's safe to assume that the show either promoted the sale or kept the sale from being stolen by the competition.

Check for media activity after the show. Add up the space you received from the public relations generated at the show and compare that to what it would cost to run an ad in the same publication. Most companies find that editorial copy out-pulls advertising copy by five to one. So, to be fair, multiply that cost number by five to get the real value of the tradeshow's ability to generate media exposure.

Try to poll visitors after the show. Ninety days after the show, grab a random stack of leads and give these people a call. Simply ask them, "Did you buy?" If they bought from the competition, you know the show was good, but your product or sales force wasn't doing the job. If they didn't buy, it gives you some indication of the market place. Either way, you'll learn if the show attracted buyers or not.

About six months after the show, poll your manager about his overall satisfaction with the show. Have show expenses, sales figures, media coverage numbers, and after-show survey results handy. Make your manager happy with one show and you'll go to almost any show you wish.

## Secrets to Success

Get more ideas now. See http://www.rxselling.com for examples of other unconventional weapons and tactics for increasing your business.

# Mark S. A. Smith

Mark S. A. Smith, *America's Trade Show Coach*, shows you unconventional weapons and tactics to meet more people, get more leads, and close more sales at your tradeshow. He's co-author of *Guerrilla Trade Show Selling* and *Guerrilla TeleSelling: How to Get the Business When You Can't Be There in Person*, and forthcoming *Guerrilla Negotiating: Unconventional Weapons and Advanced Tactics to Gain a Fair Advantage in an Unfair World*. He's published more than 300 articles on sales and marking tactics and is contributing editor to *Potentials in Marketing* magazine. He's a member of The Guerrilla Group Inc. delivering the bestselling *Guerrilla Selling Seminar* nationwide.

Bring Mark to your next event for a custom keynote, breakout session, full or multi-day training bootcamps. Reach Mark at MSASmith@rxselling.com or fax 1-800-626-7497. For more information check out http://www.rxselling.com

# Other Publications by Mark S. A. Smith

To order call 1-800-488-0780. E-mail MSASmith @rxselling.com. See http://www.rxselling.com for the latest products available and price updates. Add $US4.95 per order for shipping, $US9.95 outside of the U.S.A. Price and availability subject to change.

**Guerrilla Trade Show Selling**

"Get a copy for each of your exhibit staff." *Guerrilla Trade Show Selling* is a fast-paced, idea-packed, quick-reading book describing what you need to do, say, and think about to meet more people, get more leads, and close more sales at your next trade show. By Jay Conrad Levinson, Orvel Ray Wilson, and Mark S. A. Smith. Published by John Wiley & Sons. ISBN 0-471-16568-9. $US19.95.

**Audio Cassette Programs:**

**Trade Show Secrets: Making them Pay Off for Your Business**

A complete success strategy for your trade shows. Here's a sample of what you'll get: Learn about – and avoid – the six deadly trade show sins, things most exhibitors do that severely limit their sales. How to pack your exhibit with people who want to buy, and buy now. Three ways to get your hottest prospects to search for your exhibit. How to get the exact information you need from your visitor. Automatically spend time with visitors that can buy from you now. What to say and do with visitors at the show. How to develop your own follow-up system to close more business after the show ends. Double-length cassette. $US29.95.

**10 Things Most Companies Do at Trade Shows that Don't Work and How You Can Fix Them**

It's a crime! Eighty percent of companies that exhibit at trade shows do things that are ineffective, self-centered, or downright dumb. Learn the biggest barriers to trade show success and how you can turn your next trade show event into the best show ever! Includes hot, new ideas for every aspect of your trade show marketing campaign. $US14.95.

**7 Steps to Trade Show Success**

Here's the seven steps you must take to make your trade show work for you, instead of against you. You'll learn about Connect QUICK, the simple system that lets you get the most leads from your trade show. Plus you'll learn how to keep your energy high and feel great even after a long day on the show floor. $US9.95.

**5 Ways to Make Your Trade Show Pay Off Big**

Learn the five reasons why most companies waste their leads and how to avoid them. Why proper lead management is your best investment. How to uncover the truth about buyers. The magic five-step sequence that converts leads to sales. Six ways to get visitors to open your information package. Five ways to make money from your leads. $US14.95.

**5 Secrets that Make Your Trade Show Exhibitors Happy**

If you or your association produces trade shows as part of your events, this program is for you. Specifically designed to help association executives partner with their exhibitors to have the best exhibition ever. Recorded live at the Colorado Society of Association Executives meeting. $US9.95.

**Customers Look for You: Unconventional Marketing that Works!**

Learn why technology is making it harder to reach customers than ever before. Find out about the four marketing approaches used by rapidly growing companies and how to make them work for you, the two secrets to master marketing to the year 2000, and the two tactics that guarantee your marketing is successful. $US14.95

**Connecting With Your Customer: How to Do Business When You Only Have a Minute**

You'll learn how to connect with a stranger, understand and avoid the reasons why people won't do business with you, and break through barriers. Learn how to start conversations that are meaningful, and how to make people remember you. $US14.95.

**How to Write Letters That Make Your Phone Ring**

Guerrilla Direct Mail Marketing expert, David Garfinkel reveals the easiest, most powerful system available anywhere to produce letters that make your phone ring. Learn the 10 magic words that make your readers eyes stick to the page "like glue." And learn the one missing piece that when added to a technically perfect letter that didn't work, suddenly brings it to life and makes it a "sales champion on paper." $US14.95.

**Get More Business, Just By Speaking!**

Here's the secrets of finding more business by speaking to groups of business people. They want to hear what you have to say. How to find them, what to say to them, how to get business from them. And it costs you nothing! $US14.95.

**How to Make Audio Tapes that Increase Your Business Fast!**

How would you like a perfect salesperson to be selling for you, whenever and where ever your prospects want to buy? Audio tapes let you create the perfect salesperson. This program shows you step-by-step how you can make your first audio program for about $US25.00 using things you already own! Learn how to create titles, how to get started immediately, and how to take the next step to having your perfect salesperson working for you 24 hours a day. $US14.95.

**How to Create Information Products, Fast!**

Here's the secrets of packaging what you know. You'll learn how to produce your own audio and video tapes, books, and many other products that increase your profits. Find out who will buy from you, what to create, how to price it, and how to get it to them. Double-length cassette. $US29.95.

**Create Video Demos that Sell You!**

American Speakers Bureau executive, Frank Candy reveals how to create an outstanding video that sets you apart when people see it. With this tape, you'll learn the secrets to find a video producer that brings out your uniqueness, professional secrets to looking great on-camera, how to avoid the traps that destroy the value of many video demos, packaging that gets your tape viewed. Double-length cassette. $US29.95.

**Get More Engagements with Speakers Bureaus**

American Speakers Bureau executive, Frank Candy reveals how to get regular speaking engagements through speakers bureaus to add thousands of dollars to your bottom line every month. Learn how to get the bureau's attention, how to establish a long-lasting relationship, what bureaus and meeting planners look for, avoiding the traps that destroy a speaker's reputation, speaker media kits that get results, but don't cost you a fortune, which type of bureaus to never do business with. Two cassettes. $US29.95.

# Tradeshow Planning Essentials

by

**Jim Obermeyer**

# Tradeshow Planning Essentials

## Jim Obermeyer

This chapter breaks down the steps to producing a successful tradeshow into three sections – planning before, during and after a show.

## BEFORE

## Space Contract

One of the first steps in preparing for a tradeshow is signing the space contract that spells out exactly what management provides and for what you are responsible. Major things to look for in the contract include:

*Booth Location, Number and Size*

Selecting space can be difficult. Most show-management companies use a priority or point system. Some calculate the number of years in the show, others include booth size, association membership or financial sponsorships. Regardless, when your time comes to choose space, there are a few things to remember.

1.  There is no good or bad space. For instance, many people pass by front spaces in an effort to get to the heart of the show first. Many people start at one side and never make it to the other end, so outside aisles may not be best either. The point is – it's not important where you are, but how well you use your space.

2.  Consider physical obstructions, such as structural columns, ceiling height, fire-hose cabinets, electrical block houses, etc. Consider the power location (floor or ceiling) and where it comes out of the floor. Also, consider any windows and how ambient light may affect product demonstrations and graphics.

3.  There are no hard and fast rules about audience traffic patterns. It depends on the audience makeup. Pick a nice wide aisle and use your promotions to draw people to your space.

### Deposit Requirements

The space rental fee probably will be broken into three or four payments spread over a six-month period. If the show is in the early part of the year, you may make payments in the previous year. Be sure your budget is set up to differentiate payments for the following year's show budget. Your company's calendar year may differ from the show calendar.

### Regulations

Regulations govern what you are allowed in the space. Primary regulations deal with the maximum height allowed, use of hanging signs, maximum decibel levels, etc. Read the regulations carefully to ensure your plans do not violate rules. Violations can be grounds for removal.

### Deadlines

The contract also spells out deadlines for service order forms, shipping information and promotional information. Other key dates are the target inbound date (the date your truck should arrive), setup dates, show dates and hours, dismantle dates and target outbound dates.

If you have questions, call show management before you sign the contract, or see your company legal officer. You are signing a legal contract.

## *Booth Modification*

Depending on the space size and configuration, you may need to modify your exhibit property. New product launches, changes in product message and demonstration style may also dictate change in the exhibit or to the graphics. Make changes while the exhibit is at the warehouse, not at the show floor.

# Show Service Orders

## *Tradeshow Services Coordination*

Show paperwork is an important yet time-consuming aspect of tradeshow participation. All tradeshow services are ordered through the show manual provided by show management. In order to ensure a smooth-running installation with minimal unbudgeted expense, fill out all the show-services paperwork and coordinate all service arrangements as soon as you receive the manual. Timely processing allows you to take advantage of prepayment discounts as well as alleviate late charges.

## *Installation and Dismantle Labor Supervision*

Consider hiring a trained labor supervisor to oversee installation and dismantling. Many companies have developed strong working relationships with halls and unions around the country and provide skilled labor for your installation crew. Ask the labor supervisor for an estimate. Actual show dates, location, venue, individual city labor rates and installation times all play a part in determining the cost.

## Warehouse Handling (In and Out)

Part of your show cost is for the exhibit house to prepare and load your exhibit onto the show-bound truck, and upon return, inspect it for damage and missing parts. Before shipping, crates are opened, checked and cleaned, and the parts box is restocked. The fee for this service is insurance against expensive problems arising at the show site.

Incoming exhibits are typically opened and inspected as a quality control step at the warehouse. In addition to verifying that exhibit properties are in their proper crates, the crates are inventoried to make sure that no components are damaged or missing.

### *Exhibit Maintenance*

To extend the life of your exhibit, your exhibit house should perform regular property inspections and prompt repairs of even minor damages. It should provide you with a complete report on exhibit condition, along with repair cost estimates, when an exhibit is returned to the warehouse. All exhibit repairs should be performed to the same high standards as the original construction.

### *Shipping / Freight Carrier Selection*

You can save money by using common carriers, which normally take longer than van-line service. However, when time is critical and tradeshow transportation experience is a must, the van-line option may be the best. Van-line transportation is direct – from

origin to destination non-stop. Common carriers may
have any number of transfer points along the line. Van
lines that have tradeshow divisions are familiar with
the procedures involved in delivering to convention
centers during set-up periods.

As a last resort, when time is the only criterion,
air-freight service can be used to make a deadline, although this is expensive.

### Destination Addresses

When shipping, you typically have two options
for final destination: advance drayage warehouse and
direct show shipment.

*Advance Drayage Warehouse*: Ship in advance to
a holding warehouse in the show city. The show contractor manages the warehouse and delivers the
exhibit materials to your booth in time for the targeted
installation date. Get your shipment to the advance
warehouse two to four weeks before installation begins. Although you pay for storage at this warehouse,
it may be less expensive than direct shipment to the
show.

*Direct Show Shipment:* This shipment arrives at
the convention center on the target inbound date. The
driver checks in at a marshalling yard and gets in line
to unload. The earlier he arrives, the sooner he can
unload and the sooner your installation team can begin installing the booth. The truck is unloaded along
with all others arriving on that day. The advance drayage warehouse material is usually transferred the day
before setup is scheduled to start.

### Target Inbound and Outbound Dates

Most shows develop a target for each exhibit's
shipments to arrive. Each exhibitor is given a target

day and time when trucks should check in for unloading. This schedule is based on your location in the hall – exhibits farthest from the loading area are unloaded first, and so on.

If you miss your target, you typically are charged as much as 50% surcharge on receiving shipments. This includes late shipments of literature, graphics, product parts, etc. Basically, any inbound shipment that misses the target will be surcharged. Many shows follow the same system for the dismantle and load out. First in (farthest from the dock doors), is usually last out.

## Consolidated Shipments

When your exhibit house books transportation, you are given a date of shipment from its location. This is the day the truck is scheduled to pick up your materials from its facility. For literature, premiums, products, etc., to be consolidated with your exhibit as one shipment, send the material a few days prior to its ship date. Because some facilities charge a flat fee per inbound delivery (plus the charge per hundred weight), it makes sense to consolidate your materials.

## Damaged Properties

The more shows you attend, the greater the chances for loss or damage. What if something is damaged and you suspect it happened on the show floor after the shipment arrived?

- Read the general contractor liability information in your show kit. It details the terms under which the contractor accepts liability, as well as the limits of how much it will pay.

- Go straight to the exhibitor service desk as soon as you discover the damage. Speak to the person in charge and explain the situation in detail, then ask what recourse is available.

- Ask other exhibitors if they know anything.

- If the contractor refuses to take responsibility, pursue your claim with show management. It has more leverage with the contractor and may help you argue your case.

- Pursue litigation as a last resort. Under $1,000, it may not be worth the time or trouble.

*Insurance*

Your certificate of insurance states that you have sufficient insurance to cover materials and staff, and relieves the convention center, show management, and show contractor of any unreasonable liability.

To issue a certificate, the company needs the dates and name of the show, booth number, address of the show site and booth configuration. Add any equipment in addition to the standard configuration.

Get copies from your insurance carrier and forward them to show management. Also, verify that you are insured for the transportation of the exhibit material. Most carriers only settle for a small percentage of the actual value of the loss.

## Staff Logistics

*Staff Preparation*

In addition to a preshow training session, there are many things you can do to prepare the staff. Prepare and send a show kit consisting of material and information essential to participating in the show to every participant at least two weeks prior to the show.

Use a pocket-guide listing show staff, hours in the booth, and their product specialty. Create a staff schedule to ensure that each member has time out of the booth. If there is a dress code, be sure it is communicated well in advance of the show. For uniforms, collect sizes and order the clothing, two per person, well in advance.

## Housing

Keep the following in mind while booking hotel rooms:

1.    Most show-management companies make arrangements with the local convention and visitors bureau for special rate packages. Check the show service manual for the housing form. The disadvantage is that you may not have a choice of hotel. The housing bureau will put you wherever there is room.

2.    Negotiate with hotel properties by using existing corporate agreements. Don't expect rates to be much better. If it's a large convention, the hotel has no motivation to reduce their rates.

3.    If possible, select the host or headquarters hotel. You will be with many of the attendees, which makes it easier to meet after the show.

4.    Consider getting at least one suite. If your room block is large enough, you may get the suite for the price of a standard room, but the housing bureau won't help. Negotiate this with the hotel directly.

## Transportation

Start transportation planning early. Again, the service manual has information on airline rates with a selected carrier. It's worth checking out. Also, find out if your corporate travel group has arrangements with specific airlines. Travel planners recommend splitting up on two separate flights. It's a morbid thought, but putting your entire management team on the same plane can be a major risk.

Check into transportation from the airport to the hotel and convention center. For rental cars, team up four to a car. Again, special rates may be available from a show management supplier. Be aware that many frequent travelers will choose the airline, hotel, and rental-car company that gives frequent traveler points. Cost may not be their first priority.

*What to Take*

Contact List – The list should include your shipper, exhibit house, local exhibit houses, staff hotel rooms, home office, regional sales office and I&D account person. Leave a duplicate copy back at the office.

Critical Papers – Take essential items such as exhibitor's manual, a copy of the original space contract, paperwork documenting special arrangements and copies of service order forms. Also, bring a shipping schedule, case and contents for every crate in the shipment, a duplicate set of setup drawings and exhibit photographs.

# DURING

## Product Presentations

Live presentations can attract visitors. For the best results, research reveals that a combination of elements (live talent, video, sound and lighting) used to support a common theme holds the audience's attention and gets the message across.

## Private Meeting Areas

Each meeting area should be equipped with your product so that you can give private, in-depth demonstrations. Consider requirements for your product, furniture, power and telephone, catering and refreshments and logistics such as making and keeping appointments, sales staffing and transportation between the booth and meeting room.

## Information/Registration Area

Use the information and registration area to greet visitors, collect leads, dispense literature and premiums, make appointments, take messages and manage staff schedules. Provide power for lead imprinters and a telephone line. The cabinet should be lockable, so you can store information and materials.

## Lead Collection

Each show uses different lead-collection systems – credit-card imprint systems or automated scanning systems. Your central point of lead collection should be at the information desk.

## Premiums

Dispense premiums from a central point to ensure visitors have met requirements to receive them. When used, and when legal in the state where the show is held, contests and raffles also can be coordinated from this central point.

## Storage

Plan storage use carefully. Storage space may contain literature, premiums, audio/visual equipment, spare product, etc. Plan ahead to minimize the amount of space required. Send only the literature needed, keep spares to a minimum, if possible.

## Exhibitor Tool Kit

As you prepare for the show, have a supply of show items and office supplies on hand. Consider what office supplies, specific show items, and general show items will be necessary.

## Staff Management

Your well-trained staff needs to be managed. It's your job to coach them, manage schedules, ensure compliance with booth etiquette and protocol, resolve conflicts and motivate. Hold a 15-minute meeting each morning to review the previous day's results, restate objectives, make changes or adjustments, and answer questions.

## Competitor Research

This is an excellent time to examine the competition. Sit through a presentation, look at products, pick up literature, and ask questions. They are doing the same – count on it.

## Peer Group Networking

The tradeshow managers at other exhibiting companies are not your competitors – they are your peers. While you may work for companies that sell competing products, you are all interested in a successful show. You can influence decisions made by show management, force changes in unfair labor practices and enjoy the camaraderie of being in an exciting industry.

## Show Management

Develop a good working relationship with key people in show management. Get involved in exhibitors' committees or start one. Most committees consist of experienced exhibit managers and/or marketing personnel.

## Show Services

If you have set up direct billing, just sign and return any invoices. If you are using a company credit card, make sure it has a limit to cover the expenses. Also, confirm outbound shipping arrangements with your carrier and confirm the return destinations for the exhibit and any products not returning with the exhibit. Once this is settled, you'll get a bill of lading for each destination.

## AFTER

## Exhibit Tear Down

Once the show closes, pack your products first. If you're not completing the tear down the evening the show closes, pack and label your equipment anyway. If security is an issue, rent a security cage or hire a security guard. For literature and premiums, pack and seal them tightly or give it to a local sales office.

Confirm the destination of the exhibit with the dismantle supervisor. Before leaving, confirm that final invoices have been paid.

## Shipping Addresses

Confirm correct shipping addresses. Each destination requires a separate bill of lading and piece count. Each piece within each shipment should have at least one shipping label attached. Larger pieces should have two.

## Evaluation

Evaluating participation requires a few steps.

1. Develop a staff survey to collect information from the people who saw the show firsthand. Try to distribute this before the end of the show.

2. Plan a postshow meeting about two weeks following the show to review survey data, explain show objectives and ask for further feedback.

3. Prepare a show report outlining initial objectives, the theme and the results achieved. Your success will help senior marketing staff justify maintaining a strong tradeshow program.

4. Once the invoices have passed through the system, compare the budget to the actual expenses. Evaluate large differences.

5. Compare the initial objectives to the results achieved. Were the objectives realistic? Should they be refined? How did the show compare to previous shows?

## Staff Recognition

Reward staff members who supported your tradeshow effort. This means not only those at the show, but those who contributed to the planning and production. The objective is simple, rewarding is one way to be sure you get the best people back again.

## Billing

Once the show is over, track your final costs and compare them to the estimates projected earlier. Keep a running history of show expenses for planning each new event.

## Closure

To wrap up your participation, evaluate the show's success by asking yourself if the show was a success for the company and if you plan to return. Make any changes in the exhibit and budget. Learn from each show and you'll improve the success each time.

# Jim Obermeyer

Jim spent 13 years in corporate tradeshow and special-event management before joining Hamilton Exhibits in September of 1993. From 1993 until September 1997, Jim's primary responsibility was consulting with the company's clients to create and implement successful tradeshow marketing and sales pro-  grams. He also managed the company's sales force and directed internal and external marketing and sales support efforts. In September, 1997, he relocated to St. Louis to manage the expansion and growth of that office.

Jim was a Trade Show and Events Manager for Electronic Data Systems Company for two years. Prior to joining EDS, Jim spent 11 years as Trade Show Manager for McDonnell Douglas Corporation, producing shows and events in North America, South America and Europe.

Jim has lectured at Ball State University and Indiana State University on "Trade Show Marketing's Role in the Corporate Marketing Mix," and has presented to groups at the Exhibitor Show, Trade Show Exhibitors Association, Business Marketing Association, International Association of Business Communicators and Sales & Marketing Executives International on tradeshow marketing topics.

Jim holds a degree in Journalism and Marketing from the University of Kansas.

# HAMILTON
# EXHIBITS

The competitive forces of a changing world are raising all of our expectations to much higher levels. At Hamilton Exhibits, we know you are under pressure to produce greater tradeshow results with shorter deadlines and tighter budgets, yet the solutions are more complex and costly every day. You are continually searching for ways to get full value for every dollar you invest in tradeshow and event marketing.

Our primary objective is to assist you in maximizing the return on your tradeshow investment. We feel that a successful exhibit program requires attention to detail at every level of involvement. We believe we have created quite possibly the most potent combination anywhere of full-service program support capabilities, technologically innovative systems products and world-class custom exhibiting concepts and designs that build business.

Our total solutions tradeshow approach is built on four basic business areas: Exhibit Productions – custom and system exhibit design and production; Event Marketing – tradeshow and event planning and consulting; Program Support – logistics, field services, installation and dismantle, warehouse services and technology implementation; and Display Products – resale of portable and table-top displays, internally produced graphics, rental and lease options. Our company has been designed to provide optimum solutions and outstanding service at all levels of involvement in your tradeshow program.

We have set our sights on becoming America's benchmark for excellence in all aspects of tradeshow exhibiting, because we believe our clients expect and deserve nothing less. We have pulled together the talent, resources and entrepreneurial commitment required to deliver on this vision.

For more information about our services available to help you improve your tradeshow return on investment, contact us at one of the locations below:

9150 East 33rd Street
Indianapolis, IN   46236
317-898-9300
317-898-9353 FAX

4045 Lakefront Court
Earth City, MO 63045
314-209-9420
314-209-9424 FAX

www.hamilton-exhibits.com

SUCCESS

# Secret #4

# Measurement: Enhance Decision Making and Measure Objectives

by

Skip Cox

# Measurement: Enhance Decision Making and Measure Objectives

### Skip Cox

*"We all have a tendency to use research as a drunkard uses a lamppost for support, not for illumination."*

The point of this quote by Dave Ogilvy is obvious. Too often measurement and research are thought of only as a means of justifying budgets or proving a point in a defensive or reactive posture, rather than proactive. Today's tradeshow and event-marketing manager needs better and more predictive information to help make key strategic and tactical decisions about his program. Measurement can be a valuable management tool to reduce risk and increase levels of success if used in this way. Measurement is more than just gauging bottom-line results.

Later in this chapter we will discuss the various specialized tools available to measure specific show objectives (e.g., Sales Conversion Surveys, Pre/Post Surveys, etc.). Although these tools give some insight for decision making, they are primarily intended to measure results against objectives.

The real cornerstone of any measurement program, however, is research that provides feedback to enhance the decision making needed to plan for and improve performance in future shows. Generally this requires some form of postshow survey of attendees, one that provides the following:

- A comprehensive profile of the demographics, quality, activity, wants, needs and expectations of attendees.

- A detailed measure of exhibit performance relative to competitors and other exhibitors in the show.

More and more show organizers are providing profiles of their attendees. The value of their data in decision making and planning varies depending on the specificity of the data as it relates to your needs, i.e., how well it defines your target audience and their needs, expectations, etc. For full value, exhibitors may need to supplement show management's data with more detail about their target audience. The responsibility of measuring exhibit performance obviously belongs to the exhibitor.

## Tradeshow Decision-making Process

The tradeshow decision-making process, as illustrated in **Figure 1**, can be generally categorized into five broad areas. Decision-making begins with the most strategic of all decisions, show selection. It ends (or begins, depending upon your perspective) with deciding how performance can be improved at the next event. At this improvement stage, previous decisions may have to be refined or changed. It is a process of continuous improvement.

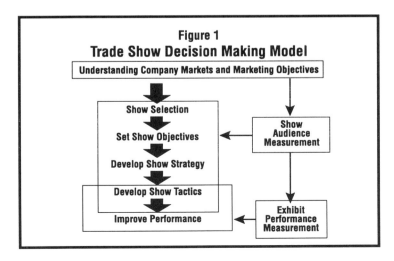

**Figure 1**
**Trade Show Decision Making Model**

Understanding Company Markets and Marketing Objectives

Show Selection

Set Show Objectives ← Show Audience Measurement

Develop Show Strategy

Develop Show Tactics

Improve Performance ← Exhibit Performance Measurement

The process begins with having a good understanding of the markets your company is trying to reach, and of your corporate marketing objectives. Effective decisions must be in line with corporate objectives and markets. Understanding your corporate objectives and markets also ensures that your exhibit program is an integral part of the marketing mix.

Show Audience Measurement and Exhibit Performance Measurement are both instrumental in making these decisions. A comprehensive profile of the audience gives the background and direction for making decisions relating to show selection, setting realistic and relevant objectives, developing a show strategy and identifying the best tactics to execute the strategy. Exhibit Performance Measurement provides feedback to help refine exhibit tactics and identify ways of improving performance.

## Show Selection

The decision to exhibit, and the level of investment you are justified in making, is based primarily on the size and value of your target market at the show. Ideally, this requires having a comprehensive profile that defines the show audience in the same way your company defines and segments its markets. For some companies this may simply require basic audience demographics. For others it may require more sophisticated audience/market segmentation criteria.

Other factors to consider are the level of interest in seeing your products, the buying influence level of the audience for your products, and the activity level of attendees relative to the size of the show (e.g., number of hours spent viewing the exhibits). The latter is important in determining the degree of difficulty in competing for the time and attention of your target audience.

## Setting Show Objectives and Show Strategy:

Understanding attendees' backgrounds, interests, expectations and reasons for attending the show are essential in setting relevant show objectives and developing a strategy for achieving those objectives. To be successful, objectives must be relevant to the needs and wants of attendees. For example, if a significant segment of the audience attended primarily to evaluate and compare products for future purchase, then sales-related objectives (e.g., obtain leads, closing sales from those leads) might be the primary reasons for exhibiting.

If, however, the attendees are higher level management who are less interested in evaluating and comparing specific products and more interested in trends and seeing what is new, then communications objectives (image building, branding, awareness building) may be the primary emphasis.

Generally speaking, the mix of sales and communications objectives should vary depending on the profile of the audience and their reasons for attending. In developing a show strategy, one of the key considerations is deciding which products, services or solutions to exhibit and emphasize. The demographic profile of the audience provides some insight to make this decision. Another key piece of information is product interest data. Obviously, products, services or solutions with the highest levels of interest should be emphasized.

## Develop Show Tactics:

Tactics developed to execute show strategy are generally based on the types of objectives set. For example, sales-related objectives generally require tactics more conducive to one-on-one interaction. This allows visitors to obtain the specific information they need to evaluate and compare products for purchase. Communications objectives are more often achieved with "one-on-many" techniques (product demonstrations, stage presentations, etc.). Therefore, the information used to set objectives and strategy also helps develop show tactics.

Background information about the wants, needs, expectations, interests and profile of the target audience is extremely valuable for refining tactics to selectively attract the best and most prospects, and to satisfy their specific needs. For example, this type of information can provide valuable insight to determine preshow promotion copy, theater presentation content, and type and mix of booth staff needed. It can also be valuable in training staff to prepare them for meeting the needs of the target audience.

## Improve Performance:

Performance improvement begins with measurement. It cannot be improved unless it is first measured and benchmarked. Exhibit performance measurement should be designed to isolate and evaluate specific exhibit tactics and elements of your exhibit (e.g., booth staff, theaters, demonstrations, promotions, visitor quality, cost-per-visitor reached, etc.) so that individual strengths and weaknesses can be identified. Also, the measurement program must evaluate all functional aspects such as traffic flow, layout, ease of finding products and information, graphics and booth size. Identifying weaknesses will lead to improved performance in the future.

Comparisons against competitors and other exhibitors will provide benchmarks. It is also an effective learning tool in identifying techniques and tactics that work for others.

## Measuring Performance against Objectives:

Enhancing decision making should lead to improved results. Measuring against well-defined show objectives is essential to determine if intended results are being achieved. Following is a discussion of the essential elements of setting measurable objectives and the measurement tools needed to track results against these objectives.

- ESTABLISH RELEVANT OBJECTIVES:

  To be relevant, objectives must be *Realistic, Specific*, and *Measurable*. (It is surprising how few companies set objectives that meet these criteria.) Furthermore, they should be written down. Out of a representative sample of about 1,500 sales, marketing and senior executives across the country, only three out of 10 managers utilized written objectives for their exhibits. This information, according to a recent study conducted by Deloitte & Touche Consulting Group for CEIR (the Center for Exhibit Industry Research), *The Power of Exhibits II*, demonstrates how under-utilized written objectives are.

  Other studies have shown higher numbers of managers (from 45% to 75%) as having show objectives, but upon closer look, these objectives are often not committed to writing, nor are they specific and by not being specific, such objectives are usually not measurable. Management may set an informal objective such as, "We want to increase awareness of our company and enhance our image at ABC Expo," but this is neither specific nor measurable. On the other hand, an objective such as, "To make 25% of our potential audience aware of our new line of personal computers" is an objective that's both specific and measurable.

Writing a realistic objective means having experience in measuring against objectives, and having a track record on which to look back. As exhibitors enter the discipline of objective setting, this may need to be a best-judgement exercise in the beginning. As a history of performance builds, realistic objectives can be written with growing confidence.

In short, written, measurable objectives become the focus for directing the planning and preparation of the exhibit, as well as defining the criteria for measuring success. This focus will drive the purpose of the exhibit. And, the higher the degree of effective objective-setting, the higher the degree of success the exhibit will enjoy in terms that are quantified, clearly understood, and thus usable for future planning.

- SELECTING MEASUREMENT TOOLS TO FIT THE OBJECTIVES' FRAMEWORK:

    The Deloitte & Touche study for CEIR quantified the percentage of exhibitors who find each of the following types of objectives very important to tradeshow exhibiting. Companies had many other objectives for exhibiting, but these are the objectives that most closely align with overall corporate marketing objectives.

    - 63% Promote Company Capabilities/ Awareness
    - 51% Introduce New Products
    - 46% Sales Leads from New Prospects
    - 36% Sales Leads from Present Customers
    - 31% Enter New Markets
    - 21% Generate Immediate Sales Orders
    - 16% Public Relations

In looking at the types of objectives exhibitors set, there are two families of objectives: communications-related (those that promote image/awareness, introduce products, PR) and direct sales-related (those for entering new markets, generating leads, generating immediate orders).

It is also evident from looking at these results that many exhibitors set both communications and sales-related objectives. This complicates the measurement function because no one-measurement tool is suited to measuring all types of objectives.

The chart titled Measurement Tools for Various Exhibiting Objectives (see **Figure 2**) illustrates the need for multiple measurement tools if multiple objectives are set. Down the left side of the chart are typical objectives exhibitors set. Across the top are various measurement tech-

| Figure 2: Measurement Tools for Various Exhibiting Objectives | | | | | | | |
|---|---|---|---|---|---|---|---|
| Objectives | Analyze Leads | In-Booth Visitor Surveys | Post-Show Attendee Surveys | Pre/Post-Show Surveys | Sales Conversion Surveys | Lead Tracking Systems | Press Coverage Analysis |
| *Communications:* | | | | | | | |
| Messaging | | √ | √ | √ | | | √ |
| Image/Branding/ Awareness | | √ | √ | √ | | | √ |
| New Product Introductions | √ | √ | √ | √ | √ | √ | √ |
| Public Relations | | | | | | | √ |
| *Sales:* | | | | | | | |
| Generate Leads | √ | | | | | | |
| Generate Sales | √ | | | | √ | √ | |
| Enter New Markets | √ | | √ | √ | √ | √ | √ |

*Down the left side of the chart are typical objectives exhibitors set. Across the top are various measurement techniques. A check mark in the matrix where an objective and measurement tool intersects indicates a tool for measuring that objective.*

niques. A check mark in the matrix where an objective and a measurement tool intersect indicates a match, i.e., a tool for measuring that objective. Following is a brief discussion of each measurement tool as it relates to measuring specific types of objectives:

## Analyzing Leads

This is generally an automatic first step of any exhibit measurement program. In addition to counting and analyzing the quality of leads, this type of analysis gives some indication of success for new-product introductions (number of quality of leads for new products) and effectiveness in entering new markets (number/quality of leads in the new markets). This analysis may also give you an indication of future sales potential by qualifying visitor buying power and intentions as part of the lead-qualification process.

## In-Booth Visitor Surveys

These types of surveys are best conducted by personal interview as visitors exit the exhibit. They are often used to evaluate the effectiveness of specific aspects of the exhibit (demos, theaters, booth staff, etc.). But as it relates to objectives, they are particularly effective in measuring message recall and retention (both unaided and aided recall). This assumes that visitors have had no prior exposure to messages. If so, a pre- and postshow survey methodology is required (discussed later). Awareness for new-product introductions can also be measured using in-booth surveys.

## Postshow Attendee Surveys

These surveys are the cornerstone of an effective measurement program. They provide a comprehensive profile of the show audience (for show selection, level of investment, and planning decisions) and they measure the performance of specific aspects of the exhibit compared to competitors (to improve performance).

Similar to in-booth surveys, they can be used to measure specific messaging and new-product introduction objectives. They can also identify through analysis of audience and visitor profiles the effectiveness of the show and your exhibit in reaching new markets.

## Pre-/Post-attendee Surveys

A pre-and postshow survey technique is required to measure message, image, brand and/or awareness objectives if attendees have had the potential for being exposed to your messages, products or company prior to the show. The preshow survey conducted prior to the show establishes a benchmark level of awareness before exposure to your exhibit, and the postshow survey measures the success of your exhibit and related activities in changing awareness, image and/or recall of the message.

## Sales Conversion Surveys

These surveys measure the dollar volume of sales resulting from leads generated by an exhibit. They're usually conducted approximately two to nine months following the show depending upon sales cycles of the products. They also measure purchases from competitors, the degree of influence the exhibit had on the purchases and the level of follow-up received from salespeople or representatives.

## Lead Tracking Systems

The ideal and most cost-effective method for measuring sales resulting from leads is a closed-loop lead-management system. Sales-conversion surveys are an alternative for companies that cannot institute a lead-tracking system due to lack of management support, channel of distribution structure (i.e., sell exclusively through dealers or distributors), inability to get field sales to report back, etc.

Both the sales-conversion survey and lead-tracking system are bottom-line oriented measurement tools. That is, they measure sales objectives, but give little explanation for results. For example, if sales are poor, is the reason the show, the exhibit, the follow-up or a combination of all factors? A comprehensive postshow attendee survey will generally provide the reasons related to the show and/or exhibit performance.

## Press Coverage Analysis

Obtaining press coverage is an objective for a relatively small number of exhibitors by comparison to most other objectives. To measure PR effectively requires follow up to determine the amount of coverage that's obtained in trade and business publications as a result of exhibiting in the show, the tone of the coverage (positive, negative, neutral) and the content of the coverage (were key messages or new products mentioned?).

- **BENCHMARK SHOW RESULTS IN ORDER TO PROVIDE A MEANS OF COMPARISON:**

    There are two ways of comparing the company's exhibit performance. Compare it either to its previous shows or its competitors' performance. Monitoring the competition's show behavior and examining its performance scores is a way of determining what works and what doesn't as well as learning more effective ways of exhibiting.

- **KEEP BASIC MEASUREMENTS CONSISTENT FROM SHOW TO SHOW, AND TRACK THEM THROUGH TIME:**

    Measurements will vary as show objectives change from year to year, but an exhibitor must try to keep the basic "metrics" consistent so that audience profile and performance can have continuity of measurement from one show to the next. This continuity is important for measurements that quantify the value of the audience and define the size of the potential audience. If tracked over the long term, the information compiled will be invaluable in selecting the best shows, and allocating the program budget amongst them.

## Measurement Works

In summary, measurement can provide much more than justification for exhibiting. It is the tradeshow and event marketer's companion to making good decisions that will lead to improved results, and to a better return on investment.

Most exhibitors have multiple objectives for exhibiting that require multiple measurement tools for assessing results. Objectives need to be specific, realistic and measurable, and must be relevant to overall corporate marketing objectives. Measuring meaningful show objectives that are relevant to corporate marketing objectives is the best way to demonstrate the value and importance of tradeshows in the marketing mix.

# Jonathan M. (Skip) Cox

Skip Cox is President of Exhibit Surveys, Inc., a full-service research and consulting organization devoted exclusively to the exposition and event-marketing industry. The company pioneered the field of exposition and event-marketing research and offers a complete range of measurement and research services to all segments of the industry – exposition and conference organizers, associations and individual exhibitors and suppliers to the industry.

Skip has literally worked in all phases of Exhibit Surveys, Inc.'s business from starting in the mailroom as a high-school student to becoming President. He served as Assistant Survey Director, Survey Director and Vice President before becoming President in 1994.

Skip's most notable early contributions to the field of exhibit research were his studies of exhibit memorability, including an analysis of the factors that contribute to that memorability, and the effect of booth location on exhibit performance. Currently he focuses much of his attention to the development of new diagnostic tools that enhance the strategic and tactical decision making of exposition and event organizers and exhibitors.

He has been a frequent contributor of articles in various trade publications and academic journals serving the marketing and events marketing fields. As a speaker, he has been invited to present the company's research findings to annual meetings of the Computer Event Marketing Association, Trade Show Exhibitors Association, Health Care Exhibitors Association, Professional Convention Management Association, International Association for Exposition Management, Society of Independent Show Organizers, National Association of Consumer Shows, American Society of Association Executives, Canadian Association of Exposition Managers, Exhibitions and Event Association of Australia, Mexican Association of Professionals in Fairs, Exhibitions and Conventions (AMPROFEC), Business Marketing Association and the Exhibitor Show.

7 Hendrickson Avenue
Red Bank, NJ 07701
Phone: (732) 741-3170
Fax: (732) 741-5704

## 1998 MARKS THE 35th ANNIVERSARY OF EXHIBIT SURVEYS, INC.

Exhibit Surveys, Inc., founded in 1963, is a full-service research and consulting organization devoted exclusively to the tradeshow and exposition industry. Our company pioneered the field of exposition research and is responsible for the development of unique diagnostic tools. Our methodologies have been tested and approved by many of the top corporate market research departments in the world.

We have a full perspective and depth of knowledge of the tradeshow industry. This is based on our years of experience in this specialized field and our work with both corporate clients and show organizers who represent a broad spectrum of industries. We have provided our quality research to more than 100 of the Fortune 500 companies and we have evaluated more than 2,000 tradeshows and more than 8,000 individual exhibits.

Our data is accepted in the industry as highly credible and extremely reliable. Our years of research have set industry benchmarks. Our metrics have become the standards of the industry and we continue to be regarded as the leader and innovator in our field.

We offer a complete range of measurement and research services to fit the individual needs of exposition and conference organizers, associations, and individual corporations. From development of the initial questionnaire, through in-house computer processing to final report, we provide professional, personalized attention and service to our clients.

We maintain the largest database of audience demographics and exhibit performance statistics for reference and comparison purposes.

We have recently entered into an alliance with Market Survey Centre (an Australian research company) to form Exhibit Surveys Pty. Ltd., which will enable us to provide research and measurement services for the growing exhibition market in Australia and Asia, including Singapore, Hong Kong and Japan. We continue to maintain our European business alliances.

SUCCESS

# Secret #5

# Managing the Show Manager

by

Sam Lippman

# Managing the Show Manager

### Sam Lippman

*"Exhibitors don't realize the power that they have."*
(A show manager with more than 20 years experience.)

## Sleeping Giants

Until recently, exhibitors in the United States were discouraged by show management from seizing opportunities to increase their own competitive advantage. Most show management was done by associations that answered to unpaid boards of directors. These volunteers were experts in their fields, but not necessarily knowledgeable about the tradeshow industry and running successful shows. The associations and their show managers were more attentive to the attendees than the exhibitors. For example, let's compare two shows: the National Computer Conference (NCC), run by a group of associations, and COMDEX. NCC, the largest U.S. computer tradeshow from 1975 to 1983, responded to the attendees' interests, disregarding the fact that the exhibitors were almost the entire source of income to these associations. In contrast, an entrepreneur started COMDEX in 1979 catering to exhibitors. By 1985, NCC was defunct and COMDEX was on its way up, becoming the largest information technology tradeshow in the world.

It wasn't until the late 1980's that exhibitors began to treat show managers as contractors. Tradeshows did not have strong competition, and did not invest in large staffs. Even dominant tradeshows used a "Jack of all trades" approach – the show manager did everything from exhibit sales and marketing, seminar planning and production, to attendee promotion and registration. It was not uncommon for a show manager to personally announce the show, send the exhibitor prospectus, take in applications, assign booth space, conduct attendee acquisition, and perform operations. Miraculously, these duties were performed on time and within budget but any new ideas competed for the show manager's time, resources, and expertise.

Another contributing factor discouraging exhibitors from leveraging show management, albeit a subtle one, is that tradeshows are by their very nature unique. Ideas and practices for one show may not be easily transferable to another. A show in Chicago in June is impossible to compare to a show in Las Vegas in January because the differences have an impact on the management of each show. This is true even if the two shows reach the same market. It is the exception rather than the rule when two shows overlap either in time or location, and exhibitors have a choice forcing show managers to compete for clients.

To this day, exhibitors do not spend the time, attention, and resources on show management that is proportionate to their investment. Exhibitors spend 25% of their tradeshow budget to rent exhibit space, according to the Center for Exhibition Industry Research (CEIR). Yet they spend just enough time with show management to reserve a space, and pay for it. The bottom line is that show managers are contractors and should be engaged as any contractor would be. An advertising agency, for example, is chosen after careful review and selection. The client/provider relationship then continues to the end of the contract period as the client approves account representatives, advertising campaigns, and deliverables.

Closer to the tradeshow industry, another analogy would be to look at an exhibitor's continuing oversight of their display builder. Exhibitors devote substantial time and effort to choosing a display builder and managing the design and construction of their displays. Why not spend the same amount of effort in choosing a tradeshow?

The method many exhibitors use to choose a show is much less structured. First they hear about the various shows by word of mouth and they canvass some of their customers to see shows they attend. Then these potential exhibitors call for prospectuses, floor plans, and applications. If enough of their competitors appear in the exhibitor lists, they complete the applications and send in the deposits. Some exhibitors even delegate show selection to their advertising or marketing contractors. Interestingly, many companies that would never select a major supplier based on word of mouth, would never take the first price offered without negotiation, and would never award a large contract without maintaining considerable oversight over the contractor, do just these things when selecting a show and signing a contract with a show manager.

## A New Era, A New Vanguard

The tradeshow industry is changing, and changing quickly. A host of factors – market forces, globalization, technology and education – is bringing sophistication and structure to the industry. "Convergence" in the tradeshow industry means increased competition. Increased competition for exhibitors means a radical change for many show managers. More tradeshows are owned and managed by for-profit show management companies. These companies invest in staff and services as a competitive advantage. The result of this increased competition is the "roll-up" of smaller tradeshow management companies into the global giants. Because of this change, even the most conservative association-based show managers are being driven to become more "exhibitor friendly."

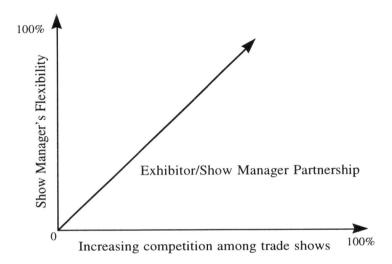

In this changed climate, exhibitors now have the opportunity to "manage the show manager." The ideal process is one in which a world-class corporation, while choosing an international tradeshow, would take the following steps:

- Send out a request for proposal to show managers,

- Ask to see marketing plans, review in detail the mailing lists, advertisement placements and public relations campaigns,

- Negotiate the company's complete image at the show, from the booth to sponsorship and banner opportunities, to speaking and media placements for key executives.

During negotiations with show managers, successful exhibitors set conditions in order to achieve their business goals. These conditions may include requiring objective third-party research about the show and audited attendance numbers. The final negotiations on price per square foot and payment schedules should be addressed after all the other items are hammered out.

In this new environment of competition, show managers have different levels of flexibility. The show manager who owns his own local bridal show can make whatever decision he feels will most help his bottom line, which, of course, is profitability. The show manager who works for a national association with strategic partnerships with other association-run shows does not have the same flexibility to respond to a single exhibitor's request.

Individual show manager characteristics are also important, such as training and education in managing tradeshows, experience and knowledge in the show's industry, amount of responsibility and authority in managing the show. The structure of show management – internal approval chain, length of time needed for a decision to be reached, budget authority, individual performance measures, and size of company – is also a contributing factor. Knowing the answers to these questions is an advantage to building better partnerships with show managers.

Now turn the magnifying glass on the exhibitor and the exhibiting company as the customers. Is the exhibitor the "squeaky wheel" or a member of the silent majority that never engages the show manager? Has the exhibitor been managing the company's tradeshow program for many years and understands the ebbs and flows of a tradeshow, or is he inexperienced, working an international megashow for the first time? Is the exhibiting company about to be downsized or is it the market leader? The type of exhibiting company and personal style and experience of the exhibitor is just as important as the show manager's style and experience.

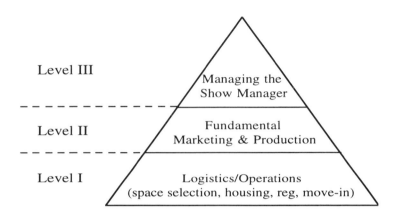

## Tips for Maximizing the Exhibitor/Show Manager Partnership

Here are some tips for exhibitors to get the most out of their relationships with show management.

*Level I*

1.  Send in space applications as soon as possible, with complete information and deposit, and thorough instructions on the desired booth configuration, including preferred surrounding and remote exhibitors.

2.  Complete all promotional opportunities: directory listing forms, matchmaking service, exporting information, "hotlinks" to web pages.

3.  Distribute guest tickets supplied by show managers to best customers and prospects.

4. Send press kits to the newsroom.

5. Visit the show manager's office on-site. Make introductions, describe your company, and offer suggestions for how the next show could be improved upon to better meet exhibitors' objectives.

## *Level II*

1. Be proactive. Promote the exhibit before the show. Use the show's logo in advertising, on your web page, and in mailings to customers, stating, "Visit us in booth XXX."

2. Reserve early advertising opportunities in the show daily, directory, banners, and billboards.

3. Order mailing lists of prior or preregistered attendees and send them a benefit-laden offer to visit booth.

4. Send press releases to the media in advance of the show, announcing what is new and different in the booth.

5. Schedule a press conference at the show to secure a press conference room. Do this early to get on the editors' calendars.

6. Enter exhibitor or product competitions that will be featured at the show. Winners get additional exposure via the show daily, special signs, ribbons in the booth, and additional listings in the directory. The media may also cover this news for months after the show. The investment in time and dollars is minimal compared to the potential return.

7. Debrief the show with show managers. Schedule a meeting after the show when performance results have been tabulated. Challenge show

managers to review their performance in attendee acquisition, new markets realized, media attention, etc.

## Level III

1.  Meet with show managers at least one cycle in advance (six months for a semi-annual show, 12 months for an annual one) to brainstorm strategies to improve the show. Bring show management and exhibitor teams together, preferably away from the show. Have your company exhibit manager meet the operations person from the show staff. Company market research people and international sales executives should meet with their counterparts in the show-management company. These teams should communicate throughout the buildup to the show and hold periodic meetings to ensure the exhibitor and show manager are still focusing on the same goals.

2.  Develop and implement a coordinated attendee/ buyer acquisition campaign with the show manager. Decide which new or existing markets need to be penetrated and design strategies that complement each other. Remember, your customer is the show manager's attendee.

3.  Use co-op targeted mailings. Share key customer lists with the show manager on a confidential basis. Use these valuable lists to negotiate for additional promotion or mailing costs from the show manager.

4.  Reach out to international attendees. Tell show managers the geographic regions that interest your company. Offer to sponsor receptions with the show manager in tradeshows and events in these regions to gain "mind share" and the de-

sire to see your booth when these buyers come to the show.

5. Design a new special event at the show that provides a benefit to the majority of the attendees. Describe the benefit to other exhibitors, and propose this event to the show managers at least one cycle prior to the show.

6. Coordinate show and industry research with show managers. Exhibitors and show managers both invest time and money surveying their various constituencies including attendees, non-attendees, exhibitors, non-exhibitors, media and international visitors. Identifying in advance, research areas that overlap and are non-proprietary, means both can benefit by working together.

7. Create and share with show managers a "sight and sound bite" in the booth. Help the trade and consumer media to "spin" this news and make company executives available for interviews.

8. Volunteer key technical and executive staff for the educational programs. Tradeshow research reveals that seminars influence what is bought on the exhibit floor.

9. Co-locate shows. If there are too many shows in an industry, do not exhibit at all of them. Ask show managers to work together if there is sufficient overlap of interests, audiences and exhibitors.

10. Consider switching to a new show. If the exhibiting company is a market leader, is unhappy with its existing tradeshow, and wants to reach new buyers who attend another show, control the outcome. Reach out to the competing show manager

several years in advance. Begin discussions to see if there might be a fit. Share your long-range strategic plan; create a campaign and then implement that plan together. This can be as aggressive as buying advertisements at one tradeshow to promote attendance at the other show, or as passive as testimonials in the new show's exhibitor prospectus.

Understand that show managers have many constituents, such as other exhibitors, attendees, facilities, contractors and unions. Show managers almost always attempt to do the most good for the most people. Exhibitors are focused strictly on their own objectives. A successful partnership between an exhibitor and a professional show manager occurs when both parties can define the area in which their interests overlap. Once that common ground is found, both parties should try to enlarge it without the exhibitor losing focus and the show manager losing sense of fair play.

## Conclusion

As competition increases in the tradeshow indus-

try, the show manager's willingness to be managed also increases. For-profit multi-management show companies now run some tradeshows that used to be run by associations. Certain tradeshows that used to be standalone are now co-located. These changes enable aggressive, proactive exhibitors to more easily partner with show managers. Exhibitors must understand that the value of their business to show managers reaches beyond the amount of square footage taken. Market leaders that have the hottest new technology or are respected in a category have leverage with show managers. This leverage helps to convince the show manager that partnerships with their exhibitors benefit all parties and ultimately the tradeshow itself.

Tradeshows have to be an integral part of a company's total marketing program. The marketing program is a symphony that plays all year long and the tradeshow is one instrument. More instruments are available now than ever before. Live event marketing is becoming a science with its own college courses. Companies, such as Nintendo, can take their products directly to the consumer with kiosks in shopping malls. Nike has dynamic retail stores in major cities and Xerox is taking control of its face-to-face marketing efforts with its own global event called DocuWorld. The Web is offering companies an inexpensive and immediate way to contact customers and prospects with product information, pricing and support. The smart marketers are adapting and changing the music they play. The show managers who want to be a part of this music will encourage their customers to "manage them."

# Sam Lippman

Sam is Vice President of the Graphic Arts Show Company (GASC), overseeing megashows such as PRINT/ CONVERFLEX USA, and GRAPH EXPO, as well as a number of regional shows for the graphic communications industries. He is also a lecturer of Advanced Topics in Trade Show Management at the Northern Virginia Community College. Four years ago, he joined GASC after spending 10 years as Vice President of the Consumer Electronics Shows, managing not only CES winter and summer, but also forging new shows such as High End Audio and CES Mexico. Sam cut his trade show teeth on the National Computer Conference from 1980 to 1984, introducing the computer industry to the Office Automation Conference.

A veteran of trade shows, conferences, and conventions of all sizes, Sam has been a front runner in building new businesses, bringing trade shows to the public, and introducing the industry to new and creative ways to enhance productivity and to become better business partners. He has worked with all aspects of the industry to build teams and negotiate highest returns on investment for all participants.

Also a teacher at the college level for six years and an international speaker, Sam is an avid proponent of better education for and about the trade show industry. He was recently presented with an IAEM merit award for his contributions to the trade show industry. He is often quoted by trade publications and broadcast media about the current and future state of the trade show industry.

Sam is a graduate of the University of California at Santa Barbara. He is married to Ellen and has a spoiled Labrador retriever named McDuff.

SUCCESS

Secret

#6

# Impress the Press

## by
### Barbara Axelson

# Impress the Press

**Barbara Axelson**

What can the press do for you at a tradeshow? They can pick up your news, decide to write about your new product, listen to your targeted presentation at a news briefing, and gain an understanding of your company.

They may attend a conference session in which one of your company gurus is participating. Maybe they will notice your advertising in the show directory, on a banner, on a logo wall, or on a shuttle bus, and decide to visit your exhibit.

The tradeshow floor is ultra-competitive. Competition for press attention is comparable to running for a lifeboat on the Titanic. You really don't want to be left behind.

Who are the press? An honest answer would be all the media since there are thousands of tradeshows. But the most frequent answer is trade press, those who write for industry magazines, newspapers, and newsletters, and the broadcast media who have a "beat" in a particular area such as technology, giftware, electronics, medical, ad infinitum.

There's a belief that everyone's fondest wish is to be featured in the center column of the *Wall Street Journal* or an article in *The New York Times*. But exhibitors in most businesses want coverage from the trade press – editors who know your market and write to your customers.

The simple fact is that tradeshows attract editors. Sometimes show managers fall down on the job and don't promote properly to the press, but most of the time they do. On the other hand, sometimes exhibitors, overall, don't promote themselves well to the press. Some do a great job, a few do a terrible job, and the majority does nothing.

Everyone can do more and every company can take steps toward building constructive press relationships in its own business niche. This includes small companies that are short on funds, other companies that are understaffed, and huge companies that have so many people doing so many things that no one knows who's doing what.

When I was a trade-press editor, I was seldom impressed with exhibitor public-relations efforts. As an editor, you cannot get too much advance material and you can't be too prepared. Once you're onsite in the pressroom, you meet colleagues and others who immediately want your attention. What you want to do is grab the directory (usually unavailable until opening day) and sit down to plan your approach. A press person needs to check the press kits immediately to see what was missed in preplanning and to confirm contact names at booths. It's useful to see which companies include a good photo so you don't have to dredge one up later.

Later on, I moved to the show-management side of the business in media relations. It was there that I determined that each exhibitor in our shows had the ammunition to impress the press. Every pressroom should be a place the editors use not just to relax and grab a cup of coffee, but where they can get information and personal assistance with every question and every bit of information that they need to do their jobs. If they wanted to meet a certain exhibitor, our staff would work to set that up. If an exhibitor were looking for coverage, we'd attempt to introduce them to appropriate editors. The lesson for the exhibitor is to know your show management; your marketers and their PR staff will cooperate. Make sure you call with your questions.

## Tradeshows Are the Site of Serendipity

It's the art of the happy accident. When you exhibit (and when you attend a show), you cannot accurately predict what new business successes will occur. Research supports the reasoning that buyers attend a show not only to visit their suppliers but also to look for new suppliers. Other exhibiting companies also fall into the buyer category at many shows. With all the buy/sell tension of a show, exhibitors forget the press possibilities.

Editorial coverage is valued at from two and a half times to three times the dollar amount of paid advertising. For instance, if you spent $8,000 for a full-page ad (often a modest amount these days), you could figure a page of editorial (in a magazine charging that rate) at a value of $24,000. Editorial is perceived by the reader to be more credible than an ad that was designed by the exhibitor/vendor.

The tradeshow is structured to be a one-time marketing event and should interest the press serving related industries. Building relationships with the media, which includes trade media (appropriate to the field), business media (more general, but still related to commerce), or consumer media (widest general interest to the public), is critical to the execution of a successful tradeshow. Considering variables such as industry, size, and location, and extending to the influence in the business and/or world community of the exhibiting companies, the approach to building these media relationships differs.

Since it serves the industry of the show, the trade press is obviously familiar with the reasons a show should exist and with the exhibiting companies (who often are advertisers in many of these publications) and with the attendees (the buyers of exhibitors' products and services, who read the publications). So, the trade press has a reason to attend the event. They want to explore new products and services. They can interview exhibitors about future business plans. They can research ideas to prepare them for future editorial treatment.

## Business Press

Business press (e.g.; *Fortune, Business Week*) and consumer media (local newspapers, network news) may have an interest in the show only if they can discover information of news-worthiness in a broad sense. For instance, the Consumer Electronics Show showcases many products in areas where fresh information is always valuable on both business and consumer fronts. A housewares event provides stories for general media since every reader is familiar with housewares and thus is part of a marketplace that is the end-user for a distributor (the audience at the show).

You can provide an application story about products that the general consumer understands, perhaps using a business customer who uses your product in an application. One of the best application stories I know of came from an exhibitor at PACK EXPO who made packing materials. In its press kit, the company included an application story in which they described a famous New-York-City museum using its product to pack valuable artwork. It was a convincing "in-use" story.

Network TV wants stories with visual appeal. If a company offers a conceptual product such as software, even with monitor demonstrations, the chances of television coverage decrease because it doesn't have the immediate visual impact for the viewer at home. Products that demonstrate well and elicit a quick "Oh!" are more appropriate for news features. Sometimes radio comes into play and you need an audio hook. For instance, an exhibitor at a recent security show gained valuable coverage with its breaking-glass detector when it was able to use that familiar sound on the air.

When tradeshows provide concurrent conferences, the trade press or consumer media may want to interview speakers or expert panelists. Consumer media will want something "intriguing," such as experts who talk about terrorism or healthcare professionals who discuss equipment breakthroughs. Consider participating in the conference as your talents permit, as a session chair, a panelist, or even a keynote speaker.

## Work with Show Management

Show management should provide a complete list of all publications on which the show may have an impact. Comprehensive media lists can be developed by your own company through excellent professional source material such as Standard Rate & Data Service, and Bacon's Magazine or Newspaper Directories, which feature comprehensive information on publication circulation, niche, ad rates, and staff.

The list should be developed further through research with each entity to determine appropriate staff contact. In print media, the managing editor may be trusted to target the proper staff member for your press releases. Radio and TV contacts vary, but station news directors are usually of help.

Pursue a course of providing news to the media all year. If the press receives enough information about the show, it benefits each exhibitor because of the increased awareness factor. Show management issues releases, but these are perceived as somewhat biased. Therefore, exhibitors must partner with management in expressing their own confidence that the show is important to the industry.

## The Basics of Communication

The fundamentals of press communication are the press kit and the press conference or briefing. Each exhibitor should prepare a press kit, a compilation of information about the company and its new products or services. Kits may be simple or elaborate, low-cost or expensive, often a folder with a company logo. These can also be an eye-catching bag, a colorful envelope, a beautifully photographed cover image, or a "wrapped" piece. These are displayed alphabetically by company name in the show pressroom, which is the meeting room for the working press. This is an excellent chance to be visible to every editor who attends the show. (At large events, there may be hundreds of press representatives.)

The contents of a press kit must be understandable. Use the active voice (forget were and had and was words). Double-spaced releases, no more than two pages in length for each new product, should be complemented by a company background piece and glossy black-and white-photos or color slides of excellent quality. The line "Photos available upon request" may be added to the release, if desired. Remember never to enclose a photo that isn't top quality. An editor has to give the photo to an art director and art directors abhor bad photos. Caption the photo on the back. The exhibitor's booth number should appear prominently on either the folder or on the first page of each press release, plus a contact name of a booth staff member, preferably two. Prepare a fact sheet if you wish, but no catalog sheets.

Incidentally, ship press kits early so that they will be on display the first morning. Remember to bring extras for the editor who wanders by your booth and hasn't picked up a kit in the pressroom.

The second demand for press attention is the press conference or news briefing. This should only be undertaken to showcase important news. Ask yourself: Will the audience receive this news with interest? Does it have impact beyond one company's promotional campaign? Will reporters respond positively to the investment of their time at your briefing?

## Plan Ahead for Press Conferences

Get your time slot before someone else grabs it; invite your guests before they've made appointments. Invitations are issued to appropriate press, first in writing, second by telephone follow-up. Phone checking should be done by someone who is able to explain the elements of the conference, rather than by an assistant who may not be familiar with details.

Scheduling should take advantage of the earlier hours of the show when people are most alert. The hour should be neither too early for a good turnout nor too late for editors who may change their plans and not attend. The final day of a show is not a good choice since many editors don't stay for the entire event. The last day is also a catch up day for them after a heavy week of press conferences. A briefing should be just that – brief. Aim for 30 to 40 minutes.

Opt for either a separate press meeting room, available through show management, or a booth demo, making certain that there is enough booth staff to handle regular attendees at the same time. Use a microphone in a booth. Editors get irritable when they have to stand in a pack or walk the booth without being able to hear properly.

The adage, "Tell them what you'll tell them; tell them; then tell them what you've told them," is one basis for a presentation. Start with the importance of what will be announced and then explain (and demonstrate) the product/service; then review what you've said. Always leave time for questions. Most reporters are anxious to clarify what they've heard before they leave the briefing and most editors prefer to get it all together so they don't have to call you back. Have mercy and don't drone on and on. Provide coherent handouts filled with the pertinent facts and accessible contacts. Forget five pages of statistics, nobody cares.

Press conferences during the usual times for breakfast or lunch should serve food. But it should always be simple to consume so reporters can take notes. For example, don't serve sticky pastries or appetizers that require a sauce. Don't do lunch with soup, salad, entree, bread, dessert and on and on. It's not a progressive dinner; it's a news event. There is no need to "wine and dine" the press; they are there for business reasons. However, if a specific hospitality function is to be combined with the briefing, it should be organized as a social or networking event with the announcement as the highlight.

Planning a gift or a gimmick? Don't do it unless it's something useful, and never do it if it's something heavy to carry. Cheap briefcases are given to editors constantly and so, oddly, are cheap pens. Coffee mugs abound and they're hard to haul around. If you hand out T-shirts, make sure they're XL. And if you thought about including a gift in a press kit, review that idea. If it's something like a Swiss Army knife, some people may feel the need to collect them and tear apart a few kits.

A note about presentation: If your top executive is (let's say it) a boring speaker, do everything you can to have someone else make the presentation. Let the

VIP take a bow or mingle afterwards, or shake hands at the door as reporters arrive.

Finally, follow up quickly. Confirm that each editor has all the materials and photos needed to write the news. Thank everyone who attends your briefing.

## Build Media Relationships Continuously

Why not become an industry source for the press? Share industry knowledge and your company experts with editors. Contribute articles within a field of expertise. Stay on top of editorial schedules by requesting annual editorial calendars.

A real effort to get to know the media in the industry is an important, long-term investment. As a company introduces its products or services, the press familiar with that company will cover its news. Don't be afraid to take an editor to lunch; it's often a good idea to get away from the office so you can tell your story without interruption. Editors work long hours and are often on deadline, which means they're sometimes curt and often harried. (This is especially true for newspaper reporters and "hot" media that are inundated with pitches.) Don't be discouraged, but be sensitive to time pressures and familiar with the format of the publication.

# Barbara Axelson

Currently president of a tradeshow consulting firm, Axelson Communications, she also teaches and writes within the field.

Drawing on experience from several career tracks, she offers planning for press and public-relations campaigns, tradeshow pressroom management, press-conference consultation and administration, press/exhibitor liaison, special-events programs, and public seminar presentations.

Ms. Axelson was the special projects editor for the leading trade publication in the process control industry. Having pioneered a custom publishing program for the world's largest trade publisher, she moved into tradeshow management, where she directed the public-relations strategy for a variety of industrial tradeshows coast to coast.

Now running her own business, Axelson Communications, with the tagline "Serving the Tradeshow Business Community," Ms. Axelson lists among her clients: associations, exhibitors, tradeshow management companies, software companies, museums, and business and trade publications.

She analyzes both tradeshow and media choices for clients and develops related educational programs for companies. A prolific freelance writer, she is also a contributing editor to the leading monthly tradeshow management publication.

848 E. Anderson Dr. • Palatine IL 60067
847-991-5353 • fax 847-991-1188
Baxelson@aol.com

# Total Marketing
# for Total Success

by

**Elaine Cohen**

# Total Marketing for Total Success

**Elaine Cohen**

What is the difference between an exhibit that tradeshow attendees pass by and an exhibit filled with activity, information and prospects? What makes visitors leave an exhibit thinking, "That product will solve our efficiency problem!" instead of, "My kids will love this little flashlight."?

The answer is often a well-crafted, fully integrated communications strategy including a message-centered live presentation. Gimmicks on the show floor are nothing more than gimmicks, but when exhibitors integrate marketing and education with entertainment; the result is increased leads from an audience that remembers both your company and your message.

A professional live presentation can bring your products and services to life. By reinforcing that message through an integrated campaign that includes promotions, graphics, props, themes, AV, giveaways and other tactics, exhibitors further increase the impact and memorability of their message, leading the way to an increase in leads and sales. Correctly planned and implemented, this medium becomes more than a presentation; it becomes a total marketing approach.

The secret to this success is consistency and integration. When your staff, presentation, graphics and collateral carry the same look, feel and content, your audience's understanding and retention of your message increase. They leave with a thorough understanding of your brand, identity and corporate image as well as key information on the benefits of your product.

## Research Documents the Benefits

Independent research has documented the benefits of using a live presentation and integrated marketing approach in your exhibit. These include the ability to:

- Attract more prospects to your exhibit;

- Communicate the appropriate marketing and product messages;

- Generate three to four times the number of qualified leads that are typically generated in an exhibit without a live presentation; and

- Provide a means to qualitatively and quantitatively measure your tradeshow results.

For example, Exhibit Surveys, a N.J.-based firm that specializes in tradeshow research, has documented that a professional live presentation integrated into a strategic marketing approach is the best strategy for companies that want to produce verifiable results from their tradeshows. The company found that in addition to increasing the number of leads three to four times, these leads typically cost 70% less to close than other leads. In fact, Exhibit Surveys states that based on its 25 years of exhibit evaluation, formal presentations are the best method companies have to make visitors remember them.

"Power of Exhibitions II: Maximizing the Role of Exhibitions in the Total Marketing Mix," a study conducted by the Center for Exhibition Industry Research (CEIR) revealed that live presentations are the third most important factor influencing exhibit memorability, right behind size and product interest. But the size of an exhibit can be cost-prohibitive and product interest is usually beyond the exhibitor's control. That leaves live presentations, coupled with an integrated marketing approach, as the most cost-effective and easily leveraged methods available to most exhibitors.

## A Successful Live Presentation and Integrated Marketing Approach

The process of creating an live presentation with an integrated marketing approach can be broken into 10 major steps. These are:

1. Setting Clear Objectives

2. Identifying the Major Message

3. Creating the Right Vehicle for Your Message

4. Ensuring a Professional Appearance

5. Integration of Marketing Elements

6. Physical Integration within the Exhibit

7. Attraction of Attendees to the Exhibit

8. Motivation of Attendees to Action

9. Staff Training

10. Measurement of Results

*Step 1: Setting Clear Objectives*

No marketing campaign can succeed without a clear direction. Therefore, the first step in planning an integrated exhibit marketing program and presentation is to clearly define your marketing objectives.

Always consider the perspectives of both management and your customers. For instance, management's wish list usually includes the following:

- Obtain qualified leads;

- Take orders;

- Enhance name recognition or brand reinforcement;

- Establish a new company image; and/or

- Give customers a corporate overview, a product overview, product information, product demonstrations and/or general education.

On the other hand, customers usually want to:

- Find out what is new and different from what they already have;

- See state-of-the-art technology;

- Learn how products can benefit them directly;

- Select a supplier for a predetermined purchase;

- Find solutions to problems;

- Research product availability;

- Speak with a sales representative;

- Schedule a future appointment;

- Request additional information; and/or

- Place an order

### Step 2: Identifying the Major Message

After you have listed all of your objectives, use that information to define your major goals, including the following questions:

- What do you want the customer to come away with?

- What image do you want to project?

- What is your major message?

- How many leads do you wish to generate?

Remember, regardless of the tactics and techniques used, the main focus must be your message and goals. Many exhibitors loose sight of the message and create programs that miss the mark from a marketing standpoint. Avoid falling in love with a concept or theme until you are sure that it supports your goals.

### *Step 3: Creating the Right Vehicle for Your Message*

To create the right marketing vehicle for your message, streamline your information further by:

- Creating one brief statement that summarizes the main message;

- Condensing your message into two or three key sub-points; and

- Brainstorming to create a list of possible ways to reiterate your message in various formats, such as visually, graphically, verbally and through demonstrations.

At the same time, assess your product and how its benefits can be communicated to the audience. Good questions to ask include:

- What is our product and how can it best be displayed?

- What is the best way to understand our product: i.e., hands-on interaction, demonstration or another method?

- What have our salespeople found to be the best way to sell our product? and

- Is there a graphic or visual way to demonstrate our product's benefits?

With this information, select a style, tone and possibly a theme for your program. Be sure to take into account the personalities of the individuals who will be attending the tradeshow, your industry's level of sophistication as a whole and the image your company wants to project. Failing to correctly define the wants, needs and culture of your audience can result in a program that misses the mark entirely.

For example, whimsy won't work with doctors and other professionals who want serious information. On the other hand, technical details will not appeal to industries where the tradeshow is the first step in an extended sales cycle.

All tradeshow presentation strategies can be classified as either corporate, theatrical or a combination of the two. The corporate style is the most common and is straightforward and conservative, conveying its information in a serious manner. The theatrical style typically integrates the message into a skit, story or theme, usually with characters and elements of fun and humor. By understanding your audience, you can select the most appropriate style or combination.

## Step 4: Ensuring a Professional Appearance

The increasingly complex images and messages we are exposed to on a daily basis are upping the ante in terms of what audiences perceive as sophisticated. Many exhibitors fail to recognize that they are competing with TV, movies, the Internet, theme parks and magazines to impress audiences.

Because the expertise required to assemble a program that will be viewed as professional is increasing daily, it is recommended that exhibitors partner with **professional script writers**, graphic artists, presenters, video producers, and AV technicians for their program, preferably those with tradeshow experience. Remember your corporate image is on the line, and a bad program or a mediocre presenter can hurt your company just as much as a good program can help. (These professionals can also help guide you through the development of the strategic and tactical elements of your program.)

## *Step 5: Integration of Marketing Elements*

Now comes the creative part. Take everything you have so far: objectives, message and style, and come up with a theme and implementation plan that meets all of your criteria. It is useful to solicit a professional creative resource to tackle this part of the process, or to brainstorm with a group of co-workers you regard as creative. Elements to define include: theme, promotional activities, presentation situation or premise, collateral, giveaways, preshow promotion, exhibit/set design, booth attire, graphics or special logos and audiovisual support.

The list of techniques that can be used to enhance your presentation and program is endless. It includes set design, music, audio/visual support, graphics, product demonstrations, lasers, video walls, dancers, performance art, animation, fiber optics, illusions, animitronics and more.

When selecting techniques, make sure they support your message, and that the image of your presentation remains consistent with the image of your product and company. As a double-check, stop periodically and ask, "Will the technique we are planning enhance our message, or distract attention from it?" Eye candy, such as video, special effects and entertainment, will always attract a crowd. But unless that crowd leaves understanding and remembering your message, your investment is wasted.

## *Step 6: Physical Integration within the Exhibit*

The relationship between your stage area and your exhibit is an important consideration in setting the mood and choreographing booth activity. Key considerations here are type of stage environment and staging.

The first decision is whether to create an open or closed environment. The benefits of an open environment are that it's instantly visible from the aisle, many people can view it at one time, adds excitement to the rest of the exhibit environment and helps draw people in.

A closed environment, however, allows you to eliminate distractions and therefore enhances the focus on your message. A closed environment also gives you greater control over ambient lighting, internal lighting, sound and audio/visual. This expands your potential opportunities to use video projections, lasers and other techniques requiring controlled light levels. In addition, a closed environment can add an element of mystery and intrigue.

Presentation staging can run the gambit from simple to fantastic. However, even the most straightforward presentation requires three items: a raised stage, lighting and professional audio. A raised stage makes your presentation more prominent, increases your sight lines and gives your presenter more authority. In order to maximize your stage's ability to draw and hold attention, make sure it is placed where there are no obstructions and within easy access to the rest of the exhibit. A backwall behind the stage is usually a necessity. This ensures your audience can focus upon the presentation.

A professionally installed audio system is the single most important element contributing to your success; it ensures that your message is projected clearly and audibly throughout the exhibit. Having a professional sound technician on hand is essential in eliminating feedback and adjusting volume levels.

Lighting is another element that helps to create a vital, lively, energized environment for your presentation. Even when budgets are limited, a general stage wash and spotlighting to provide emphasis are necessary elements.

## Step 7: *Attraction of Attendees to Your Exhibit*

Next, it's time to develop a strategy to attract people to your exhibit. In order to maximize results, never rely solely on walk-by traffic to fill your audience. Instead, create a pre- and at- show promotional plan to enhance your results.

Prior to your show, generate interest in your program by informing potential and current customers what you are planning. This can be accomplished by a thematically integrated direct mail, phone or Fax program that is consistent with the messaging that will be in the exhibit. Most show managers are happy to help by supplying lists of preregistered attendees for this use. You can also advertise your program in trade journals and other industry publications, on your Web site and in your company's communications. These techniques can become even more effective when used in conjunction with an incentive, such as a prize, for attendees who view your presentation.

At the show, invite attendees to your presentation with door drops, ads in the show daily, banners in the convention center or other advertising and promotional techniques, always thematically integrated with the rest of your program for consistency. In addition to helping draw an audience, these tactics are an excellent way to reiterate your message and brand image.

Always train your booth staff to actively entice attendees to view the presentation, or if your staff is too shy, hire a professional crowd gatherer. An incentive, such as a small gift, an entry in a prize drawing or a combination of the two helps to build traffic, as do catchy promotional graphics, music and comfortable chairs to sit in while the presentation takes place.

### *Step 8: Motivation of Attendees to Action*

Live presentations can be a powerful tool in motivating your audience to action. Would you like your prospects to talk to a sales representative? Fill out a lead card? Watch a product demo? Sign up for a trial test? Set up an appointment? Place an order? It's as simple as deciding what you want them to do and setting up the right incentive. For instance, popular techniques include:

- Offering a prize upgrade for taking the next step (such as seeing the product demo),

- Distributing a game card requiring the attendee to answer questions or visit several areas of the exhibit to receive a gift, and

- Offering a discount on products purchased at or within a set time frame after the show.

## *Step 9: Staff Training*

By preparing your exhibit staff prior to the show, they will be prepared to help entice attendees into your exhibit and to view your presentation. They can also take an active role in implementing your promotional plans by helping facilitate traffic flow between the presentation and other booth activities. By watching the responses of attendees to the presentation, the staff can help pinpoint hot prospects to approach.

## *Step 10: Measurement of Results*

One of the most crucial areas in marketing, especially at tradeshows, is measuring results. Without measurement, a company has no way of tracking its return on investment or justifying its participation in a particular tradeshow.

Integrated presentations and marketing programs present several opportunities for measuring results. The easiest method is to count the number of individuals or leads (potential or current customers) generated by your live presentation. A formal lead card, filled in with the attendee's personal information and answers to several qualifying questions, can be designed to facilitate the counting and tracking process. These leads should be sorted by quality and urgency of follow up and compared to the previous year's results. Subsequent measurements can be made by following up with the sales force on a regular basis to track the number of actual proposals and sales generated by the leads.

Another method of measurement is to implement an exit or postshow survey. By including questions that gauge the audience's understanding and recall of your message, you can compile both quantitative and qualitative information.

When calculating return on investment, always try to amortize your costs by re-using your presentation at press conferences, sales meetings, customer presentations, hospitality suites, sales presentations – either live or on videotape. The more you re-use your presentation, the more value it has to management.

## Summary

When correctly planned and implemented, professional live presentations combined with integrated marketing campaigns have the best success rate of any tradeshow marketing technique. Whether your objective is to increase brand awareness, introduce a new product, or reposition your company, a live presentation can increase your company's return on its tradeshow investment.

# Elaine Cohen

Elaine Cohen is president of Chicago-based Live Marketing, the leading producer of exhibit marketing strategies and presentations. Elaine and her team of creative directors, actors, writers, scenic designers and audio/visual specialists annually produce more than 500 presentations worldwide. Their programs help companies communicate their message more effectively, increase impact and build brand image while generating three to four times the number of leads.

Their innovative products and services include presentations, thematic integration, video and multimedia, speaker coaching, consultation, interactive kiosks and more.

Elaine founded Live Marketing more than 26 years ago, after identifying the unfilled need for professional presentations on the tradeshow floor. Elaine herself is responsible for coining the term "live marketing," which in addition to being the name of her company has become the exhibit industry's moniker for live presentations.

Live Marketing's work has received numerous industry awards. More than 400 of Live Marketing's presentations have been included in Exhibit Surveys' list of the 10 most remembered presentations at their respective shows. Exhibitor Magazine has given eight of its annual Sizzle Awards to Live Marketing presentations, and four Live Marketing presentations have been key components in exhibits selected to receive the Focus Award for exhibit marketing excellence from the Trade Show Exhibitors Association.

Live Marketing also received Exhibitor Magazine's Best New Product Award in 1995 for its introduction of Thematic Integration, a service that combines a strategic exhibit marketing plan with tactical implementation. Thematic Integration integrates every aspect of a tradeshow marketing program ensuring that all elements from promotion to giveaways communicate and reiterate one consistent message.

Current clients include Cisco Systems, Eastman Kodak, Intel, Johnson & Johnson, Lucent Technologies, Motorola, Philips, Siemens and Sony. Live Marketing can be reached at 312-787-4800.

**SUCCESS**

# Secret #8

# Using Magic to Attract Attendees: The Real Secret to Success

by

**Charles Greene III**

# Using Magic to Attract Attendees: The Real Secret to Success

**Charles Greene III**

## What's Going On?

Imagine walking down a tradeshow aisle and several exhibits away you see an audience of about 20 attendees listening to a sales representative. As you approach you hear the sales rep delivering the product message in a focused and clear manner. Within moments, you know the key selling points of the product.

The audience continues to grow as you get closer. Joining them, you see that the sales rep is performing magic to illustrate the product message. "I wish our exhibit had this many people listening to our message," you think to yourself. "Lucky they had someone in their marketing department who knows how to do magic."

Before you can leave, someone hands you a packet containing a magic trick that's imprinted with the company's logo and product message. Then a salesperson invites you into the exhibit to see a product demonstration. After the tradeshow ends, you open the packet and find the magic trick includes additional product information.

## Who Was That Man?

The truth is that the company was not lucky, they were pro-active. And the presenter with whom you just spent the last 10 minutes is a "corporate" magician. He was hired to attract attention, communicate the client's product message and involve attendees with the company's exhibit program. Although this is a fictitious situation, you may have already experienced a similar scenario on a tradeshow floor.

All over Corporate America, magical presentations are being engaged to enliven logos, information and messages. Magic is a proven solution for breaking through audience apathy. But how can you gain this magical advantage for your company's exhibit program? This chapter will guide you through the process. You'll learn the essential components of adding a corporate magician to your sales team and making sure that your magical presentation delivers your information in a credible manner that enhances your marketing efforts.

## What Is a "Corporate" Magician?

A corporate magician is a magical performer who uses the art of magic and illusion as a marketing tool. When a corporate magician works, two things happen – magic is performed while a message is spoken. The spoken text has been scripted to feature a precise marketing message that includes product information, benefits and features. The subject matter could be a new tangible product, or a spectrum of intangible concepts such as faster service, high quality or better customer support.

## Why Use Magic?

Put simply – magic works. It is a proven solution. According to Exhibit Surveys, Inc., magic is the second most effective attention-getting technique for product and/or company identity. (Product demonstrations are the first.) Magic has the power to attract attention. However, to create positive memorability for your message, your presentation must go beyond mere attraction, it must have a clear message. That's where scripting comes in. With a script focused on your exhibit message, a magical presentation becomes an educational experience.

For attendees walking the show floor, all exhibits begin to look the same after only a few hours. Even if your company has a brand new exhibit, so might your competition. You may have the newest product, but if your competition has something extra that catches that attendee's attention, that's where that attendee will go. You can't show off your latest product if attendees pass your exhibit rushing to some other "destination." You need some advantage to help your exhibit stand out.

Your prospects spend time searching for exhibits that interest them. They are tuned into that old radio station, WIIFM, "What's In It For Me." A magical tradeshow presentation offers them this implicit bargain – "If you listen to my message, you'll be entertained. If you spend time in this exhibit, you'll enjoy the time you spend here." That's what attendees want. Regardless of professional educational pursuits, on a personal level they just don't want to be bored.

Magic has the power to attract people like a magnet. Utilizing that power, you communicate your product message to a willing audience. They actually enjoy spending time in your exhibit and learning about your product. The key to maximizing that captivating power is to give your audience a clear product message that they can remember.

Besides making your exhibit a "destination" and offering your message to a larger audience, a magical presentation also gives you a more motivated exhibit team. They now have a pro-active exhibit that brings them informed attendees who already know your exhibit message from watching the presentation. This saves your staff time and allows them to work with more qualified prospects.

## Making the Right Performer Appear

Magic works, but to make this presentation idea come alive you need to find a corporate magician. When you think of a magician, what comes to mind? Perhaps you conjure up images of David Copperfield vanishing the Statue of Liberty; Uncle Ernie pulling a quarter out of your ear, or even the well-worn image of a man in an ill-fitting tuxedo and a few doves. All of those images have their place, at least the first two, but not in your tradeshow exhibit.

What you want is a magician who has experience delivering scripted corporate information through magical presentations. You're looking for a conservative conjurer who has the proper balance of corporate culture and magical talent. Here's a hint: He's got more frequent flyer miles than your boss.

Your real aim is to have someone who fits in with the company image. If someone suggests a tuxedo, resist the urge. This just makes your message look like a novelty. Your corporate magician is the spokesperson for your message and should be dressed conservatively, such as a business suit and wingtips.

One place to find a corporate magician is to ask your exhibit house representative. She may have worked with one and be able to give you some special insight. Check out the resource directories and websites of trade publications and exhibitor magazines. Another resource is other exhibit managers. Ask them who they've heard about in their travels.

Perhaps the worst place to look is "The Yellow Pages." Even in a large metropolitan area, chances are you won't find what you really want by letting your fingers do the walking. A lot of magicians say they do corporate work, but this may translate into entertaining families at company picnics or the annual holiday party.

Whether you get a recommendation, or find one on your own, get plenty of information on your chosen performer. Does he have a web-site that you can visit until his promotional packet arrives by mail? Review the information closely. Call a few clients and ask about their experiences. Generally, the busier the performer, the more experienced and credible he is. Ask about his schedule. If he's doing between 20 - 30 national shows per year, you've found a winner.

You may have to present your findings to your associates, so be prepared for some skeptical looks when you say the word "magician." Tell them to keep an open mind. Show them the press articles, client lists, photos, letters of recommendations and other supporting data of your chosen candidate. Don't forget to state that magic is the second most effective attention-getting technique for product and/or company identity, according to Exhibit Surveys, Inc. (Product demonstrations are the first.)

Once enough people start believing that this is a viable option, you may, depending on your time frame, have your corporate magician visit with you and your associates in your home office and give a capabilities presentation. This gives everyone an opportunity to meet and ask questions about how a presentation works with special requests and requirements.

One word of caution – Don't rely solely on a video. Although you may receive one, videos can actually be counter-productive to finding the best performer. They are representative of only brief moments, and only slightly better than a portfolio of photographs in evaluating a live presentation. When you view a video, you're really looking at the editing and production skills of the video producer.

Once selected, let your exhibit staff know about the special presentation planned for the exhibit. Ask your corporate magician to participate in your preshow meeting. Set some time for him to inform your exhibit team on how the presentation affects them and how they can effectively "work" the audience during the presentation. This is the best time to give a brief performance of the presentation.

## What's In It for you?

Add an experienced corporate magician to your exhibit team and expect the following results:

*Better booth attendance*

From the beginning of the first day until the final presentation, you have an activity that has instant attention-grabbing power. Magical presentations are pro-active presentations that stop attendees and hold their attention.

*Multiple return visits by attendees*

When your message is communicated within the framework of a magical presentation, attendees are willing to see the presentation and hear your message more than once. They will discuss it with other attendees and return to see the presentation again and again. Each time they stop at your exhibit, they hear your message. It's not uncommon during a three-day tradeshow for an attendee to see the presentation three or four times.

*Increased message memorability*

Magical presentations place attendees in a receptive mode to hear your information. The audience watches the magic and hears your message. All the message "filters" are turned off. This means that your product information and exhibit message stay longer in the minds of your prospects. They hear the specific information you want them to hear while they are in their most relaxed, listening state.

*Greater exhibit excitement and visibility*

A magical presentation also makes it easier for your exhibit staffers to stop people and engage them in conversation. They can use the presentation to their advantage by scanning the audience for special attendees with whom they'd like to visit.

## Training Your Magician

The steps for developing a customized presentation are usually straightforward. Most people wonder, "How will he ever learn about our message?" In short, he'll ask. From your responses, a script is written. You should then review the script and make changes and revisions. The script memorized and then performed.

This process ensures that the message in the presentation remains focused and supports your exhibit program. Let's take a look at a few of the steps in the creative process.

*Input meetings* – These meetings may take place on the phone or in person. Depending upon the details and the number of people involved, the performer may visit your site to meet with your associates to give them ideas on how he can convey the message through a presentation. This is the time to talk about exhibit layout and placement of the presentation area. It's also a great time to talk about what you want your audience to do at the end of the presentation: i.e., fill out a lead card, visit with a sales person, etc.

*Proposal* – After listening to the particulars of your event, you should receive a written proposal with presentation options based on your initial input sessions. Besides outlining all responsibilities and requirements, this is where you get finalized numbers for the presentation, payment schedules and other options.

*Letter of Agreement* – Based on your selected presentation options, you should receive confirming paperwork. This contract reconfirms the details for dates (arrival and performing), location of the exhibit area, finalized investment numbers, deposits, etc.

*Presentation Outline Guide* – This is where you'll state your message. You should complete a multi-page questionnaire or a worksheet. This information forms the basis of your script. Using a structured worksheet, instead of just grabbing a bunch of brochures, helps to maintain focus on the core message that you want your audience to hear. To assist your corporate magician in learning the meaning of your responses, supply any relevant information such as exhibit copy graphics, product sheets, preshow mailer copy, annual reports, etc. With this information, and your responses to the questionnaire, your corporate magician is now able to select the best magic to support your information.

*Presentation Script* – After reviewing all of your information, your corporate magician writes a script draft of the presentation. He then sends you a script draft before the exhibit. This is your opportunity to review the script line by line and make sure that your information is being delivered properly and accurately.

If you've given lots of input and your responses in the presentation outline guide were focused, the draft should be close to the mark and should only require minor changes.

Keep in mind that the process in approving a script varies from company to company. For example: In the medical industry, the draft goes to the exhibit manager, to the product manager and to the legal department. In another industry the draft may only need to be approved by one person. Make sure that you set up an appropriate time frame so that the script and revisions can be approved well before the exhibit dates. Since this is a memorized presentation, there is nothing worse for a performer than to get the final approved script on the day before exhibits start.

## Preparing for Your Magician

*Performing area placement:* Allow enough space in your exhibit for a performance area as well as for the audience. For a theater-style presentation, you'll probably need a dedicated theater space with seats. For a standing audience, a small table and platform may be required.

The performance area should be at least 6 to 10 feet from the edge of your exhibit. This keeps the audience out the aisles as they watch the presentation. The best position is a corner, as opposed to the side of an exhibit. This will give the presentation maximum viewing exposure to the largest number of attendees. Resist the temptation to place the performing area in the middle of a 30 by 30 exhibit. Due to human nature, few attendees will venture that far into an exhibit space.

*Presentation assistant:* This should be an outside person, not a company person, who's responsibility is to welcome people to the exhibit and encourage them to watch the presentation. During peak periods, she can assist in keeping the audience inside your exhibit and prevent them from spilling over into the aisle. The presentation assistant also is responsible for handing out lead cards, magical premiums and company information.

*Magical premiums:* At the end of the presentation, you may have considered giving away a premium item such as pens, but with a little planning, you can maximize the message with a magical premium. Imagine, teaching attendees how to do a simple magic trick that involves your message and logo. Instead of just handing them a free pen, give them a premium that they can use and at the same time, extends your message far beyond the tradeshow floor.

One example is a magical premium called the "3 Card Monte." It is an easy-to-do card trick in which a playing card changes to a card with your exhibit message. Your magical performer should be able to supply you with a simple custom-printed magical effect that promotes your exhibit message.

*Sound:* The greatest magical presentation will fall flat if it can't be heard. An effective sound system ensures that even with a full audience, everyone watching can hear your performer. One or two small speakers should be enough for basic voice reinforcement. If you're planning to have your exhibit house provide a sound system, remember to order a wireless, lavaliere system. For obvious reasons, magicians prefer to have their hands free.

One word of caution, check with your neighboring exhibits and ask them to let you know directly if the sound is too loud. Sound levels change depending upon the activity of the exhibit hall. What may have been a perfect sound level at the beginning of the day may be far too loud as the hall traffic thins out.

*Investment:* For a four-day tradeshow, expect to invest several thousand dollars, not hundreds, for a fully customized and scripted magical presentation. Separate from production and scripting costs, you also have to factor in the expenses of travel and lodging. As with other aspects of your exhibit, such as carpeting, etc., you get what you pay for. Invest wisely and receive a "R.O.I." of a successful tradeshow event. Skimp, and you'll skimp alone. This is not the place to "save a few bucks." A professional corporate magician works hard to communicate your message and make it come alive. He delivers your message and keeps it "fresh" during the entire tradeshow.

Magic is a proven tradeshow presentation option. It attracts attendees, captivates their attention and, with accurate scripting, gives your prospects an educational experience. The key to true success is finding the right corporate magician and focusing the attention on your product. As with all magic, learning the secrets is not that difficult, but you need a true professional to make it easy to maximize your message and get amazing results at your next tradeshow.

# Charles Greene III

Charles Greene III is the president and founder of Corporate Shuffle, a company that provides customized magical presentations for exhibits, sales meetings and client events. From close-up magic for tradeshows to large-scale illusions for sales meetings, the company always meets the need and then  exceeds the expectations of its clients. Besides providing world-class magical talent for corporate events, Corporate Shuffle consults on magical marketing ideas and concepts for preshow mailers, premiums, video productions, executive programs, and training programs.

Through Corporate Shuffle, Charles travels the world. He's worked on corporate productions in Bermuda, Egypt, Mexico, Monaco and Sweden. His clients span a variety of industries and include 3M, Clorox, Frito-Lay, Johnson & Johnson, Minolta and Panasonic. His magical marketing has been featured in numerous publications including Discover, Robb Report, Training and The Wall Street Journal. He's even been quoted Reader's Digest.

In the world of magic, Charles is known as a magician's magician. He was selected as the representative "corporate" magician for a historic 50 episode television production on the history. He's appeared on the cover of the two largest international publications in the magical arts, "Genii" and "Magic." A frequent contributor to magic journals, Charles has been awarded top honors by The International Brotherhood of Magicians and Siegfried and Roy. Charles is a member of Hollywood's "Magic Castle" and of London's "Magic Circle."

*"With your presentations, we were able to increase our presence at the show and triple our leads from the previous year. You made a 'believer' out of our group."*
– Juleanne Dawson
Bard Access Systems

*"You really opened doors for us. Your presentations gave us opportunities with our clients that we didn't have before."*
– Pat Wente
KPMG Peat Marwick

*"Your expertise and professional incorporation of both corporate and product messages into your program was exactly what we were looking for."*
– Linda Possinger
Pasteur Mrieux Connaught

For more information on Charles Greene III
and his magical productions contact:

Corporate Shuffle
Phone, 800-759-5194 • Fax 800-217-5568
or visit the Corporate Shuffle
web-site: www.CorporateShuffle.com
e-mail: info@CorporateShuffle.com

YOUR MESSAGE • OUR MAGIC • AMAZING RESULTS

Make your company's product information and marketing message the center of attention. Let Corporate Shuffle weave your sales message into a customized magical presentation that will captivate, communicate and educate.

Our presentations break through audience apathy and place your message on center stage. As Citicorp experienced, "Your ability to draw crowds in, capture their attention and then turn it to out products was a joy to watch."

Besides additional attention, you'll increase your message's memorability. We'll work with you to custom-script a magical presentation that educates viewers about your product line. Corporate Shuffle's years of work with even the most technical products have made us experts at tailoring illusions to specific products or services.

Give your company a magical advantage. Call

**800-759-5194**

today to receive your FREE exhibit marketing packet or visit our website:

**www.corporateshuffle.com.**

# 7 Steps to Exhibiting Success

by

Susan Friedmann

# 7 Steps to Exhibiting Success

**Susan Friedmann**

If your idea of exhibiting consists of buying space, showing up and reacting, then you're playing a dangerous game of "Russian Roulette" with your economic future. You may be successful, but that's questionable. Why take a chance when a little extra effort can mean guaranteed positive results?

Let's assume it's the first day of the show and your team is now ready to do its job. (Assuming all preshow planning and promotion is taken care of.) Your staff's job is to represent your company or organization as an ambassador. In other words, they are a "microcosm of the macrocosm." Everything and everyone in the company is being represented on the show floor, from the president to the receptionist. An attendee's perception of your company will be swayed by his experiences with your representatives. Let's hope it's a positive one.

Any visitor to your exhibit forms an opinion of the company the moment he steps onto the rented carpeting. He may come armed with certain expectations if he's heard of the company. Quite simply, booth staff can make or break these impressions based on their attitude and behavior. Eighty-five percent of a visitor's impression about your exhibit is determined by the staff's attitude and behavior, according to tradeshow research conducted by Incomm International. In addition, 80% of a final buying decision can be influenced by your booth interaction

Therefore, this is not something that should be taken lightly. That is why is it so important to find only the best staffers to fill your exhibit. Unfortunately, too many companies fail to realize the importance of tradeshows, fail to put the needed time and effort into them and then wonder why they are not getting results.

This chapter covers seven essential steps for you and your team to use in order to maximize the time spent on the show floor. These steps, for simplicity's sake, are the seven steps that spell *SUCCESS*.

## Step 1: S – Start with a Positive Image.

It is important to quickly break down any barriers to create a positive impression and build rapport between you and the attendee. How long does it take to create a first impression? Seconds. Various surveys state anything from 10 seconds to 30 seconds, none of which are very long. But in that short time, you can be judged on body language and appearance quite easily. You've probably even done it yourself.

To create a positive first impression, follow the seven key points below:

**1:** Smile. It sounds simple, but smiling is a universal language. A smile can automatically put people at ease.

**2:** Good eye contact is essential and conveys honesty and trustworthiness. Even children have a hard time keeping eye contact when telling a fib.

**3:** A good solid handshake tells it all. Beware of the "wet noodle" handshake, which conveys a weak and unsure character, or using both hands, such as the "politician's handshake" or the "glove," using both hands around your hand. The two-handed shake, where a person shakes with one hand and places his hand around your elbow area, and the glove handshake, both smack of insincerity. Remember that a single solid handshake is sufficient.

**4:** Greet positively. It is important to acknowledge the attendee's choice to enter your exhibit in the form of a thank you. People like to be appreciated.

**5:** Introduce yourself. This seems obvious but many people forget to introduce themselves while trying to remember to give specific company information.

**6:** Insist on a dress code. Mandate either a company uniform or strict dress guidelines. Although it may sound like this should be low on the priority list, it can make a big difference in first impressions.

Recently, just before a tradeshow, executives for an exhibiting company issued a memo instructing everyone to wear "dark" suits in the booth. Interestingly, men interpreted this to mean black, brown or navy, women were even less strict and found beige to navy in the realm of "dark." The message is simple – spell out a specific list of what is acceptable before the show begins. For example, let men know the color of suits, shirts and ties that are acceptable. For women, what color blouses and accessories need to be outlined.

Uniforms are not only "in," they are the easiest way for you to control what your staff wears. Casual golf or polo shirts with an embroidered logo are the most popular uniform items regularly seen. Corporate ties, scarves or vests are also popular. The company budget and image will dictate what works. And don't forget to consult staff members. Some may have very strong opinions about uniforms that will need to be addressed.

**7:** Remember, clients are everywhere. It is critical for your team to realize that whatever they do or say, on or off the floor during a show, is reflected on the company. People will form an opinion just as quickly on an elevator after show hours as they will in an exhibit during show hours. This is especially true if uniforms are used in the booth. The advantage is that everyone knows where you work. The disadvantage is that everyone knows where you work.

## Step 2: U – Uncover the Attendee's Identity.

Most attendees wear badges, but don't rely on them for accurate information. As you probably know, attendees can borrow badges from other people to get on to the show floor.

Use a simple greeting, such as, "Welcome and thank you for coming to the ABC company booth." Shake hands and continue. "I'm Mary Smith, president and owner of the company and you are...?" Once you know his name, find out what company he represents and ask, "What exactly do you for them?" Make your interaction friendly, but get as much information as possible since time is of the essence.

Did you know that 68% of the people walking the show floor are part of a buying team? According to research conducted by the Center for Exhibition Industry Research (CEIR), it's a fact. These groups usually have a plan and know exactly which booths they need to visit. They may split up to find specific information, then meet later.

Be aware that tradeshows are also one of the most overt environments for espionage. A competitor can easily wear someone else's badge to get information. Fortunately, most competitors are very good at giving themselves away. They either ask questions that are too technical or involve details the average attendee would not ask. Train your staff to only answer relevant questions. For example, a response to a very technical question could be, "That's interesting you should ask that, what specifically do you need to know?" or, "How would this information help your particular situation?" Get the attendee to do more talking. This will be covered in more detail shortly.

## Step 3: C – Create a Conversation.

As mentioned above, there is just a small window of opportunity to find out who the attendee is, where he is from, what he is interested in and why, tell him about your products and services and follow up. Actually, you have just 3 to 5 minutes on average, to get through this with a smooth, relaxed and informative demeanor. Simple, right?

And now the 80/20 rule comes into play. Quite simply, during that 3-to-5-minute window of opportunity, 80% of the time should be spent listening, and 20% conveying information about your products and services.

Of course, this rule of thumb is not always followed. Without fail there's one booth staffer who talks too much and listens too little. He comes on strong, gives information galore and never inquires about the attendee. This is called "throwing up" on the attendee. Not a pretty sight and totally useless.

The key to a quality conversation with an attendee is determined by the questions asked. In workshops I conduct frequently, participants are encouraged to spend a great deal of time deciding on the best questions to ask, based on the information needed. (See ExhibitSmart Series booklet, "62 Questions to Qualify Your Prospect.")

First, try to cover all areas if you're unfamiliar with the attendee. These include his present situation, what he's looking to change and why he's looking to make these changes. Also, cover the time frame for this change. Find out who's involved in the decision-making process and the budget? The last thing you want to do is spend time talking to someone about a product or service that is completely out of his price range or control.

What product is he currently using? Find out what he likes about it and what, in an ideal world, he would change. Remember, if it is a competitive product or service, don't knock it! It's bad business and a put-down to the person who bought it. Rather, find out how your product can better serve the prospect.

To do this, practice "active listening." Be totally present to the attendee and involved and interested in helping him improve his current situation. Keep a close rein on that little voice inside your head waiting to jump in and take over the conversation. Act in a consultative mode so that you can capture the attendee's concerns.

### Step 4: C – Capture the Attendee's Concerns.

Through your questions, constantly listen for how best you can help him, while keeping in mind that time is not on your side. That may be why it is too easy to skip questions and cut straight to the "throw-up routine."

Over the last few years, more and more exhibitors have been leaning toward the European style of exhibiting. Establishing a relationship with clients and prospective clients is the key, and for that reason, European stands usually include a conference area – a more intimate place to invite key customers or hot prospects to spend quality time. Some companies even have special presentations in these areas that are by invitation only.

## Step 5: E – Empathize and Show Understanding.

People like to do business with those they like and trust. After you spend time creating the conversation and capturing the attendee's concerns, let him know that you truly understand his situation. In fact, if it is one that you are very familiar with, tell him. But, never lie. It is not worth it. Just prepare to embark on the next step, which is to find a solution to his problem.

## Step 6: S – Search for Solutions.

If you've asked the right questions by now, you should have plenty of information to make your presentation or demonstration. In other words, it's time to do your thing.

Remember that the best demonstrations are the ones that involve the attendee. Exhibiting is highly sensory and attendees are required to use their senses in many different ways – seeing, hearing, feeling and, at food shows, smelling and tasting. The more you encourage your prospects to use their senses, the more they are likely to remember you. When an attendee walks the floor and visits, on average, 30 exhibits in a day, it's tough to remember one from another.

It is for this reason that many companies go to great expense to create a truly memorable environment, including Hollywood-style live entertainment. However, live entertainment isn't going to find out what the prospect needs. It is still your job to get attendees involved in the demonstration. The more you can get him to use as many senses as possible, the better off you are. Ask how they see the company using the product and address any concerns at this point.

## Lead Cards

Don't forget the importance of lead cards during your encounters with attendees. Make notes on these cards so that follow-up action is communicated to those responsible for lead follow-up. Right now, there is no industry standard for lead cards, and therefore you may have a different lead capturing/retrieval systems for each show you attend, unless of course you invest in your own.

So what are some of the basics you should consider when designing your lead-management program? Here are seven powerful tips:

**1.** Design a user-friendly lead card. Create one that is easy for your team to complete and gives your salespeople good quality information to follow-up on after the show.

**2.** If you are going to use rented lead-retrieval equipment, make sure you know how the leads are formatted. Also make sure that you know how soon you will have those leads. Some systems can produce information instantly; others take a few days. Can you get the information on disk? Find out what it takes to integrate it into your existing lead-management database.

**3.** Prevent hand-written leads from taking second or even third place on your to-do list when you return to the office. Too many people are guilty of this, 80% to be exact. According to CEIR, that's how many leads are left without any follow up. Why spend precious money at a show with a goal of increasing sales, and then discard the key element to making those sales? Beats me, but it happens.

For instance, at a recent show in which I presented a training seminar, I walked the aisles after the seminar. I found a great ergonomic office chair in one booth that really interested me, enough to spend at least 20 minutes with the sales representative. He did everything right and promised I would be contacted shortly. Eight months later, I'm still waiting for his call.

**4.** Make sure your staff is familiar with the lead system you choose. The easier it is, the more likely your staff members are to capture the information. In your preshow meetings, spend a few moments going through the process. Make sure you and your staff can easily use any electronic-retrieval system. There should not be any surprises for any team member.

**5.** Create a prospect-ranking system to easily determine how hot the prospect is and when he is planning to buy.

**6.** Make sure there is a different follow-up plan for each type of prospect. For example, treat a prospect who is "hot" with a greater sense of urgency than someone who may be interested in including your product in next year's budget.

**7.** If an attendee offers you a business card, *don't write on it*. Why? In the United States, we don't tend to place as much value on business cards as they do in other countries. We normally don't think twice about writing a note to ourselves or taking a person's card and putting it in our pocket without even looking at it. But in European and Asian countries, a business card is like a passport. It represents that person's identity, and writing on it is just like defacing it. My general rule of thumb – don't do it at all and then you won't run the risk of offending anyone. (See ExhibitSmart Series booklet, "10 Steps to Making Your Show Leads Pay Off.")

## Step 7: S – Solidify a Commitment.

When the time comes to close the interaction, establish what the next step is going to be. The easiest way to do this is ask the prospective customer. Does he want someone to call, does he want a quote, maybe he just wants literature? Close the deal with a solid agreement on the next step. Make sure to capture this information on a lead card.

If giveaways are used, now is the time to utilize them. Using these items at the end of the encounter is very effective. It extends your thanks for the attendee's attention and offers him one more way to remember the company. For this reason, I am a true believer in giving away something of value. If it will help the attendee to better do his job, or is educational, it's a winner. Try to avoid typical pens and key chains and try to be creative.

Since 66% of literature is actually thrown away before it is even read, your company's printed material can be called a giveaway. Although attendees will keep something of value, such as a specific article reprint or study, they usually have a tendency to take stuff just because it's there. Combat this by offering an inexpensive piece that can be tossed. You can keep a few pieces of your primary literature available for attendees who really do want to take something with them.

Also, consider having press kits available both in the pressroom and at your booth for the media who will be scouting the show floor for new ideas.

It is time to bid the attendee goodbye. Make sure you have agreed on a follow-up plan. Give the attendee his gift, shake hands and thank him again.

## So Long and Farewell

The seven-step SUCCESS model will work if you follow it. Creating a positive image, finding out who the attendee is, steering the conversation and finding out what he wants is just the start. If you remember to empathize with him and find solutions for his concerns, then you're on your way to solidifying a commitment.

Tradeshows can be a total waste of time and money or they can be an incredibly powerful marketing tool that can boost your sales, reputation and credibility. The choice is up to you.

Wishing you much tradeshow success!

# Susan A. Friedmann

Susan works with organizations that want to attract new business at tradeshows and with show organizers and exhibitors who want to retain and grow their customer base.

She works one-on-one or with teams to help boost tradeshow results. She also conducts presentations and workshops for groups nationally and internationally. She provides her clients with what they need to know to attract more business by focusing on four critical areas: planning, promotion, people and productivity. She identifies and helps people develop certain skills that are critical to their trade show success now and in the future. She shows people how to build better relationships with customers, prospects and advocates in the marketplace to retain and grow their business.

Originally from London, England, Susan has been a coach, speaker and author for over 20 years. Her extensive experience in the tradeshow industry has allowed her to work with several hundred companies representing more than 30 different industries in the U.S. and in Europe.

As an innovative and insightful speaker, Susan has been featured at major conventions and in the media. An abridged version of her book *Exhibiting at Trade Shows: Tips and Techniques for Success* has been translated into French, German, Italian and Spanish. In addition, she has a video tape *The Nuts and Bolts of Selling at Tradeshows*, and is a regular contributing editor to numerous professional and trade publications, in particular, *Convene, Cintermex, Ideas, Exhibitor Times, and Exhibitor Marketing Magazine.* Most recently, she compiled and published the latest book on exhibiting, *Secrets of Successful Exhibiting.*

To find out how Susan Friedmann, The Tradeshow Coach can help your tradeshow success, call (518) 523-1320.

MEMBER

NATIONAL
SPEAKERS
ASSOCIATION

# Exhibit Marketing Systems that Work

### The Nuts & Bolts of Selling at Tradeshows

This dynamic *"how-to"* video is packed full of practical, easy-to-use information that guarantees every exhibitor more successful and profitable results from tradeshows. Watch as Susan Friedmann reveals techniques to:

- *Help you identify and approach interested prospects*
- *Provide a formula for qualifying prospects to obtain quality information for future follow-up*
- *Give you specific steps to take charge of the conversation that creates and maintains a high quality image*
- *Help you develop effective listening techniques that make every prospect feel important*
- *Eliminate spending unnecessary time with uninterested parties*
- *Communicate professional closing techniques that outline future follow-up action.*

Once you have discovered Susan's new ideas, and mastered her latest proven techniques and special skills, you will see an instant return on your tradeshow investment!

***VHS Video Cassette (20 min.)***                    ***(PAL version available)***
***Regular price:  $199***

### Exhibiting at Tradeshows: Tips & Techniques for Success

An easy read for the beginner and a good reminder for the pro.  It contains numerous easy-to-use and practical *"how-to"* strategies for successful and profitable exhibiting results. Whether you are a one-person operation or a multinational corporation, exhibit at a trade show or consumer show, a conference, exposition, or mall show, there is something in here for you. *This book is a required survival kit for every exhibitor!*

***Softcover Book (Customization available)***       ***Regular price:  $15***

### Secrets of Successful Exhibiting

From some of America's leading tradeshow professionals, this book shares useful, practical information to help make every exhibiting experience pay off - no matter what size the show, or exhibit.  Offering sound professional advice and guidance – a formula for success to master the unique, high-pressure exhibiting environment. Packed with a wealth of success strategies, tips and insights, you will find answers to many of your exhibiting questions.

***Softcover Book***                                ***Regular price: $19.95***

### ExhibiTips – The Collection

This 48-page loose-leaf manual is a collection of hundreds of practical tips and techniques on all aspects of tradeshow exhibiting from Exhibit Management through Boothmanship, Sales & Marketing, International Exhibiting and Professional Development. Learn the do's & don'ts of successful tradeshow exhibiting from marketing before the event, through working with labor unions at the show, greeting & qualifying prospects, proper exhibitor behavior, and follow-up strategies that you put in place before your prospect even leaves the show.

***Loose-leaf Manual (48 pages)***        ***Regular price: $50***

### Power Exhibiting

This audio cassette tape is a dynamic approach to quality exhibit marketing. It was developed to help exhibitors communicate a stronger uniqueness in the competitive trade show arena. You will learn how to: Master your communicating skills; Develop a successful exhibit team; Create the right image; and Boost your leads to generate profit.

***Single Audio Cassette***        ***Regular price: $19.95***

### ExhibitSmart series –
***7 Steps to Exhibiting Success • 101 Cost-Cutting Tips for the Savvy Exhibitor • 62 Powerful Questions to Qualify Your Prospects • 10 Steps to Making Your Show Leads Pay Off***

Each booklets presents cutting-edge, proven techniques that improve skills, increase confidence and get results. Perfect for those who want practical, easy-to-apply methods that will help them create a competitive edge at every show.

***Regular price: $6.95 each, the four-book set is $25***

### 7 Steps to Exhibiting Success

This powerful audio cassette tape and booklet guides you through the simple SUCCESS formula every exhibitor needs to make a difference and get results on the show floor.

***Regular price: $24.95***

Unconditional 100-day 100% Money-back Guarantee Order:

800-647-5455
Fax: 518-523-8755

# Controlling the Leads Nightmare

by
John Hasbrouck

# Controlling the Leads Nightmare

## John Hasbrouck

Although it's one of the most important reasons why companies exhibit at tradeshows, it's also one of the lowest priorities on the budget. While exhibitors spend thousands of dollars on booth design, entertainment, labor, and giveaways, the amount spent on lead management is practically nil.

Have you ever considered what percentage of your tradeshow budget is spent on leads? Most companies spend more money on drayage at one show than they do on the leads process for an *entire year* (the average is less than 2 percent!)

The problem is that it's a tough process to get a hold of. One reason for this is the ever-changing leads systems that are available at shows. Some offer magstripe card readers, others use 2D bar codes, and some even offer website systems. With so many different technologies, how can company reps learn a standard process for leads? And after the show, the frustration of dealing with the leads and getting them into a database is enough to drive a person crazy. Even though the process is a difficult mess, your boss still expects results. The tradeshow budget is more and more under fire, and an answer is needed to the question, "How much did we sell from all those leads?" A good leads system can help answer that question and keep your tradeshow budget intact, because it can produce fantastic results.

## Take Control of the Process

To establish a leads system, you need to take control of the process. Develop a system that you can use at every show, from the largest booth to the pop-up or tiny table-top display. This way, everyone in the company can learn it, depend on it, and use it. You will also be able to process your leads easily after each show and get the same quality of leads at both the large and small shows.

First, assign one person to be responsible for the specific goal of getting X number of qualified leads from the show. Try not to assign this to the tradeshow manager since he or she probably already has a full plate. Assign it to a marketing or sales manager who has something to gain by obtaining better leads.

Determine the goals for each show and for the year. These can be to get 200 qualified leads at each show for every 400 feet of booth space or to get X leads per sales rep staffing the booth. Additional goals could be to acquire 200 qualified leads from potential dealers who can carry our product this year, without mention of leads per square foot. Once you have agreed on a goal, write it down and let everyone know what it is.

## Aim for Quality, Not Quantity

"Quality not Quantity" should be your battle cry. Stop and consider what happens when the sales force gets a pile of unqualified leads after a show. These reps were already busy before the show, and now you are dumping a ton of leads on which they must follow-up. After calling the 15th or 20th lead, they often give up, complaining that the leads are lousy. You know the show went great, so how could the leads be lousy? Unfortunately, these reps give up because without serious screening or qualifications, each name looks the same. Who knows if the 21st call would have been the million-dollar buyer? To determine what constitutes a qualified lead, go right to the end user of the leads – the sales rep and/or distributors.

Ask the sales manager and reps what information they need to make a lead valuable. Information about the lead other than the name and phone number is essential. While a long lead form is impractical on the busy tradeshow floor, consider this basic information:

- Product Interest (Product A, Product B, C, D, all of the above).

- Units Needed (1-2, 3-5, 6-10, etc.)

- Purchase Authority (Information Gatherer, Recommend, Final Say, None)

- Timeframe to Purchase (Immediate, 30 Days, 30-60 days, 60- 90 days, 90 days +)

- Follow-up Request (Send Literature ONLY, Have Rep Call, On-Site Demo, etc.)

Also, plan an area for notes to add comments that might help the sales rep, such as "Cindy was just promoted and has a new budget," "Bill will be on vacation until July 12," or "Taylor needs a solution for left-handed widgets that are OSHA certified." These basic qualification areas should come up in conversation with an attendee, so completing this survey should be quick and easy for the reps.

## Software vs. Paper Lead Forms

Are you using a PC or laptop to help with the leads or just paper forms? A PC is a great tool since you can get the information turned around very quickly, and it allows you to make corrections, qualify, and take notes. Many companies that use live presentations use a combination of both in the booth. Software solutions for leads vary, from shrink wrap to custom solutions provided by companies such as NewLeads (www.newleads.com) and American Exposition Technologies (AET-www.expobadge.com).

Custom solutions are great, but can take a while to pay off. Mike Chase, a tradeshow professional with Hewlett Packard Medical, owns Trade Show Manager (by AET). The software was customized to the company's needs. "We used to get about 30 percent unqualified leads," he said. "Now it is down to 3 percent."

Hmmm, talk about sales improvement. Mike's system has the ability to directly read most of the different show badges, including magstripe cards and 2D bar codes (possible with NewLeads, as well, which also reads business cards). He has several tabs on his screen to qualify a customer according to the product-line interest.

While shopping for software, ask important questions, such as, "Can I customize this for my company or do I have to hire your programmer (for how much) each time I need changes?" Also, ask which of the tradeshow badges the system can read or are you required to rent a system to hook up to your computer? Always ask basic questions, such as how long the company has been around, does it have 24-hour support, and will it give you a list of references.

## Pre-stage the Postshow Mailing

Regardless of the method of lead capturing you choose; make sure you are ready to follow up on the leads. Consider assembling a packet of information for leads before the show. Write your thank you letter in advance, with merge fields, so that it can be customized to each person. Have it ready on disk to merge print as soon as you return. Have everything else ready and in an envelope. Print a message on your envelope, such as "XYZ Show Follow-up." When you return, merge print and sign the letters, insert specific literature, affix the labels, and send them out the door.

## Where to Take the Leads

Once you have determined the method of lead collection and are ready for follow up, determine where the leads will be taken. The information counter is a great place to handle the "information seeker," or someone who would just like your literature. According to the *Wall Street Journal*, only 25% of tradeshow literature makes it all the way home with the attendee. (Who knows how much gets read?) Darla Johnston, a tradeshow professional at Motorola Computer Group, minimizes the waste by printing literature on demand at the show, and given only to serious inquirers. First, the literature was converted to Adobe Acrobat PDF documents. Then, using an inkjet printer in the booth, literature is just a drag and drop and prints on the spot. She also owns her own lead-retrieval system (NewLeads), which runs in the background on the same laptop.

Your "quality conversation" leads should be taken throughout the booth. If a rep is speaking with an interested and qualified prospect, the rep should be able to find a leads station nearby. If you are taking laptops, or using Windows computers in your booth, put your leads software on all the machines. You can run the leads program on the same computers that are already in your booth, saving space and doubling the efficiency of the computer. (Establish a policy that you don't interrupt a demo to take a lead).

If the booth doesn't have lead stations, you risk losing many valuable leads. All too often, after a rep talks to a prospect, he then directs him to the leads counter and says, "See you later Mr. Prospect. Thanks for your time. Hey Cindy, will you swipe Mr. Prospect's card?" This is a big mistake. Can you guess what happens next? The entire conversation and information about this potential buyer just evaporated in the pass of the badge to the information counter: Mr. Qualified just became Mr. Justa Name.

For this very reason, booth staff must always enter their own leads. If someone is waiting, instruct your representative to simply state, "I'll be right with you. We should be finished in a minute or two. Is that OK?" The rep can then take just a minute to get the basic info into the leads system so as not to forget it. Going back later to enter the lead seldom works or gets the same detail and depth of information.

## Watch Out for Errors!

Relying on badge information can be dangerous. On average, 20% of all tradeshow badges are missing information or have errors. How many times have you heard "Oh, that's not my phone number!" or "This isn't really my badge." At least one badge producer rarely puts the attendee's title on the badge. What good is a lead if you don't know whether the prospect is the janitor or the CEO? To remedy this, train your reps to verify the information with the prospect after the badge is swiped or scanned. Fill in the missing information on paper or on the software program and correct the errors.

The rep should be able to easily check off the qualifiers on a lead form or on a software program. Taking notes at that moment is also OK, especially if it is specific to what a customer is asking. With software, you can go back and revisit the record of the customer to take more notes later. If you are using paper lead forms, take the printout from the lead machine, correct errors in pen, and staple the printout to your lead form.

## The Big Hurdle: Getting the Buy-in from the Reps

If you really want to change your company's lead management, you need the reps in the booth to buy in on the new system. You may even consider an outside trainer or consultant. In some cases, this person can command the attention you might not get inside your company. He or she can train your reps at the show on taking leads, booth behavior, how to sell on the tradeshow floor and many more areas. Specialists such as Matt Hill (The Hill Group, San Jose, CA), Michelle Bruno (The Bruno Group, Salt Lake City, UT) and Susan Friedmann (The Tradeshow Coach, Lake Placid, NY) are perfect for this type of training.

Be sure to spend time with reps at each lead station and coach them on the new lead-taking method. One simple system to teach is what I refer to as the GALE method. This simply stands for Greet, Ask, Listen, and then Enter the card. This differs from the more commonly used method of swiping first and asking questions later. The problem with this method is that you may have swiped the card of a completely unqualified lead (maybe even your competitor!) With the GALE method, you greet the attendee, ask about her company and what she does at the company, and how you might help her. You listen to her needs and at the end of the conversation you then enter (swipe or scan) her card and complete the information.

Keep in mind that not every lead must be entered. Your reps should be trained to recognize, within the first 60 seconds, if a person is a lead or not. Have them ask questions such as, "What do you do with the XYZ Company?" and "What is it you are looking for specifically?" If the prospect is there to talk about the good old days in the War, chances are you probably don't have a serious lead. Remember, every minute on the floor costs your company at least $10, and probably a lot more. Make the most of it!

## Processing the Leads

When the show is over, be ready to follow up these leads you and your reps have so carefully acquired. If you are using a software solution, your leads should be ready to import into your database or merge mail program. Representatives from Eastman Kodak take leads on laptops around the booth, using a survey form on each laptop. Using NewLeads Survey Builder software, these reps collect leads into one laptop at the end of each day. They then export the leads daily to a disk, which travels by Fed-Ex to the fulfillment house. These leads are sometimes printed on a report and handed to the sales manager on-site. Imagine taking care of the entire process right there. What a relief! If your reps are using software to capture and qualify leads, these leads can then be e-mailed quickly to sales representatives or the fulfillment house. Try setting up an e-mail merge letter to use at the show, using programs such as Microsoft Word or ACT! Then e-mail merge at the end of each day, and the response from attendees will be great. Include a hypertext link to your web site. The first one to the prospect often determines the sale.

## Following Up on those Leads

As we discussed, working with your sales department is a must if you want the lead-management plan to work. Talk with your sales department about the post-show plan. Discuss how long initial follow-up calls should take. Be sure to get a realistic picture of how many leads they can handle and then filter the leads you give to them if you have too many. By using a database, you can sort out the immediate and 30-day buyers from the long-term prospects.

Make sure the right leads go to the sales force at the right time. Make sure you stay on top of those leads by requesting a report on the status of the leads, two, four and six months after the show. This helps you to tweak the program to see if the reps are following up and if the show was a true winner and worth repeating. If they aren't following up, find out why.

In the end, it all comes back to management's question, "Why do we spend so much money on tradeshows?" and for once, you will have actual results to back up your answer.

# John Hasbrouck

John Hasbrouck has been actively involved in the exhibit industry since 1990, first as an exhibitor, marketing educational videos, and then as a consultant.

It is an unlikely career for someone who began as a television news reporter, covering hot spots in Central American countries like Nicaragua and El Salvador.

His switch to the tradeshow industry began in 1990, as he began marketing his own educational videos at trade shows. Hasbrouck developed solutions to the problems he encountered while collecting and following up leads.

Today, he is president of NewLeads, Inc. in Los Angeles, the premiere provider of software solutions for companies who wish to standardize and improve their trade show leads process. Mr. Hasbrouck also provides training and he design leads systems for companies needing a complete show-to-sales process. He can be reached on the internet at john@newleads.com or by phone at 877-775-3237, ext. 13.

*Frustrated With Lead Retrieval?*

# Take Control
## of Your Leads!

### 1 Same system, every show.

Swipe or scan a trade show badge, or even a business card. The lead pops right up on your PC. Correct the errors and add any missing information!

**YOU OWN IT!**

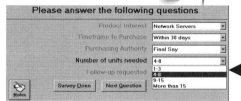

Please answer the following questions

| | |
|---|---|
| Product Interest | Network Servers |
| Timeframe to Purchase | Within 30 days |
| Purchasing Authority | Final Say |
| Number of units needed | 4-8 |
| Follow-up requested | 1-3 / 4-8 / 9-15 / More than 15 |

Survey Done    Next Question    Notes

### 2 Qualified leads.

Our expandable, multiple choice survey is just like your paper lead form. It's easy to design and use, and you can take notes at any time.

### 3 Instant leads processing!

At show's end, simply import the leads into ACT!, GoldMine, Access, Excel — ANY database! Choose from our pre-formatted reports, and even e-mail your leads from the trade show floor!

# NewLeads

*Qualified leads, instant access!*

## Call toll free: 877-77-LEADS
### www.newleads.com

179

# Working Effectively with the International Customer

by

Marcia A. Smith

# Working Effectively with the International Customer

## Marcia A. Smith

The world is getting smaller and smaller, and this has never been truer than at a tradeshow. Exhibitors today meet potential customers, suppliers and distributors from all over the world, right at the booth. In fact most tradeshow organizers encourage attendance by international firms and individuals.

So what is it that strikes fear into the heart of almost every exhibitor who greets an international customer? Is it the language? Is it the fear of cultural differences in business and customs? Is it wondering how to get paid? The primary reason most people are reticent about international transactions is that they do not understand the difference between doing business domestically and with international clients. Why? Most of us never learned what the international trade process is all about.

Global trade, as well as the industry surrounding it, involves complex rules and regulations. Many individuals may not be exposed to international markets during their education or business career, but inexperience is no reason to shy away from thinking and acting globally. International trade is not hard; it is just a different way of performing basic business functions.

This chapter presents ideas on how to work effectively with international customers – particularly those who appear at a tradeshow. There are three primary sections.

*Preshow Preparation*. Whether the company is new-to-export or a seasoned trader, preshow preparation for the international customer is vital. This section discusses simple, yet important, techniques that allow the exhibitor to proactively interact with its international client.

*At-show Presentation*. The approach, enthusiasm and genuine interest exhibitors show toward international customers is critical. In this section, you'll find easy to use techniques for recognizing and dealing with cultural differences and establishing good business contacts.

*After-show Follow Up*. Establishing a presence in the international market is important to any business. Learn how to successfully continue contacting international customers and develop a strategy for successfully opening and expanding into foreign markets.

## The International Trade Process

Before beginning a detailed discussion of each of the phases above, it is important to understand the international trade process. The four stages in the international trade process help set up what should be accomplished before, during and after a tradeshow. **Figure 1** shows how each of these stages flows.

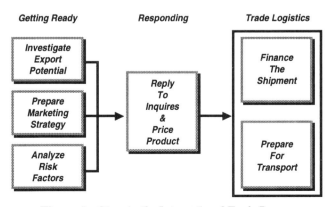

**Figure 1** – *Steps in the International Trade Process*

## Getting Export Ready

The following three areas are critical to performing an export-readiness internal audit:

1.   Investigating Export Potential

Is your company capable of handling the added tasks and responsibilities involved in exporting? Preparing a company for exporting helps management and staff to successfully compete for foreign trades. Getting ready to export prior to attending a tradeshow doesn't take a great deal of time or resources. These critical factors should be considered:

- Motivation to enter the export marketplace

- Corporate commitment and goals for domestic and foreign markets

- Pricing and distribution strategies for the international marketplace

- Commitment of extra resources and funds for developing export markets

2.   Identifying Export Markets

Whether an unsolicited inquiry comes from a foreign buyer, or a company is actively seeking to develop target markets, it is important to match the markets to the product or service being offered. Unfortunately, very few products or services are sold "as is" into any foreign market. To analyze this, consider:

- Product suitability for the export marketplace

- Modifications to the product or service necessary for overseas markets

- Distribution methods and channels in export markets

- Assessing the competition domestically and internationally in those target markets

3.  Analyzing Risk Factors

There are a number of risks to consider when going global that are not necessarily part of a domestic transaction. Some of the common risk factors and insurance that should be considered include:

- Property concerns for loss in transit overseas

- Transportation concerns for problems with packing, shipping, and documentation for foreign sales

- Product liability concerns in the foreign target market

- Personnel liability for overseas staff and facilities

## Responding to Inquiries & Export Pricing

Pricing for international trade is different from pricing for domestic sales. The 13 different International Terms of Trade (INCOTERMS) define the delivery and payment provisions. Also consider the coverage for risks and other export-related costs, such as fees, documentation and customs charges. Successfully working with foreign buyers means understanding these extra charges and how they relate to the product or service offered. Being competitive in these areas can determine a company's staying power in the export business!

## Exporting Financing

Export financing is a broad area with many different options. A number of financing instruments that are very common to international trade are not used for domestic transactions. Creatively using these alternatives can help in negotiating international trades. Some of the most common methods include:

- Cash in Advance
- Letters of Credit
- Documentary Collections
- Bankers Acceptances
- Open Account

Each of these options varies in terms of the risk and obligations of the buyer and the seller.

## Transportation & Shipping

Transportation terms, rules and jargon are perhaps the most unfamiliar part of the international trade process. With international trade, the exporter must recognize and adhere to different forms of government regulations, policies and customs. It is important for everyone to understand what is meant by the logistics of trade. Performing these functions takes training and skill, but understanding how the process works does not. You need a working knowledge of the logistics when talking with international clients. Some of these include:

- International carrier options and modes of transport
- Packing, marking and labeling requirements
- Preparation and delivery of documentation
- Insurance coverage and claims procedures
- Booking freight
- Licenses, restrictions, customs, export regulations and compliance

## Preshow Preparation for International Buyers

During the preshow stage, perform an export-readiness internal audit, analyze product suitability for foreign markets and identify several specific target markets. Define distribution strategies and be aware of potential risk factors and coverage. By following the suggested format in the international-trade process, evaluation of the important factors can result in a written international business and marketing plan. This strategic plan can drive the entire approach before, during and after the tradeshow.

Generally, it is unwise to entertain foreign business without making sure that management and staff can support it. Fulfilling and sustaining export activities may not be economically feasible without this support. Therefore, take the following steps to set up a plan:

- Define the motivation for entering foreign markets.

- Determine if this motivation fits within the company's overall goals and objectives.

- Garner commitment from all levels of the organization for exporting as a way of expanding profits, customer base and increasing market share.

- Determine what international distribution channels are best for the company currently and in the future.

- Identify resources to set-aside in order to build and maintain export markets.

- Evaluate the price structure and compensation schedule for domestic sales and develop new ones, if needed, for the export marketplace.

- Define the operational costs and support needed for foreign markets.

Also, spend some preshow time assessing product suitability and identify and analyze target markets in order to determine the following:

- Modifications necessary to sell the product in foreign markets. These modifications may be in terms of physical characteristics such as size, design, color, etc., as well as special product packaging requirements.

- Changes needed to product literature, warrantees, training materials, promotional and advertising media.

- Define sensitive cultural and social differences that may impact the acceptance of the product.

- Identify several countries or regions that have the greatest potential for export success without a high-resource commitment.

- Gather economic, social, cultural and political information about the target markets.

- Narrow the focus in those markets by identifying:

    - Demographics of consumer base

    - Consumption patterns and needs

    - Distribution channels

    - Competition for product or service

    - Restrictions or barriers

- Use the information gained from the market research to redesign product literature, promotional, and advertising materials, including translation.

- Put the English and translated message in the same document to prevent misunderstandings.

- Always have someone fluent in the native language read the materials first.

• Request a listing of tradeshow attendees from foreign countries. Send information and company literature prior to the show.

- Follow up with these foreign buyers and schedule appointments at the booth.

- Arrange for a translator to attend the meeting, if necessary.

- Research the target market, buyer and customer prior to the meeting.

• Contact potential distributors, foreign sales representatives, agents or export-management companies that can help establish the product or service. Provide company promotional literature.

- Perform basic due diligence on the distributor and/or its company.

- In the conference listing, include anyone at the booth who will be responsible for dealing with international trades. If possible, list any languages, beyond English, available at the booth.

• Using the target-market research information, as well as current market-analysis information, identify the competition and define how established it is in the foreign market.

- Analyze the product or service against those offered by the competition.

Consider the following while analyzing potential risk factors and defining coverage options:

- What level of risk is the company willing to undertake with regard to shipments to foreign buyers?

- Identify insurance carriers of packing, handling and transportation and discuss costs and procedures for these services.

- Determine liability insurance and personnel coverage costs for doing business in foreign markets.

Prepare export price lists, terms of payment and terms of commerce (INCOTERM) options. This list helps the company focus on the extra costs needed for foreign sales and defines what the company is willing to accept regarding risk coverage, finance options and shipping arrangements. The export price list is used to work with foreign buyers at the tradeshow.

## At-show Presentations for the International Buyer

Establishing a flourishing international market is no different, fundamentally, than doing business in the United States. The company and staff know their market, customers, competition and how to approach and furnish that market with goods or services. Basically, the same procedures are important for international trade. However, be prepared for differences in language, customs, and basic business practices. Let's discuss how to accommodate these three differences.

1.  Language Differences

English is the language of international business, and most international traders can speak English to some degree. But be prepared to address language differences, particularly if the product or service requires technical discussions.

- Contact local interpreters to assist in the booth, if needed, by asking show management or contacting local Chambers of Commerce.

- Some show managers provide multi-lingual interpreters on an as-needed basis while others provide international rooms with language services. Use them.

- Anticipate unscheduled visitors.

- Extend invitations to other visitors as you learn of them. Base language and translation needs accordingly.

- Define whether there will be sufficient visitors to the booth to warrant hiring an interpreter.

- If you make arrangements to have interpreters at the booth, advertise it in the booth and list all languages.

- Don't forget to pay attention a person's body language and facial expressions. Both of these are important, so be aware of the manner in which words are spoken, how they are delivered, their intonation and style, as well as body movements.

2.   Cultural Differences

Preshow research helps exhibitors deal with cultural differences. The only way to know what is appropriate and non-offensive is to do your homework. Attention to the details of cultural differences can make a foreign buyer want to do business with you rather than with the competition. Most foreign buyers have a very positive impression of exhibitors who try to accommodate them.

If, for example, there is a high proportion of Asian attendees, why not learn about Asian culture and morays? Make a good impression on the visitor, and ultimately it may be a factor in how the product or service is received. Being aware of cultural differences can also prevent major mistakes. For instance, the color white is associated with mourning in Asian culture. Also, adapting to and customizing at-show presentations does not have to be an emotionally crippling experience. Good market research helps provide awareness of the following:

- Word meanings and writing styles
- Messages and the type and form of advertising and promotional materials/media
- Living conditions, kinship patterns and family structures
- One-on-one relationships – friendship/family vs. business acquaintances
- Value of education and skilled vs. unskilled workforce
- Food and drink preferences
- Color and symbol meanings
- Quality and style preferences
- Geographical and seasonal differences
- Religious preferences, celebrations and holidays
- Display and shelf sizes, procedures for stocking and displaying
- Metric measurements, foreign electrical and other standards

Consumer products and services are subject to the most scrutiny and variation due to cultural differences. The physical product itself and the associated messages that it carries are important. For example, soap is a basic product needed worldwide. In some countries it is given in a fancy box as a gift. The meaning is certainly different than if you gave a friend a bar of deodorant soap.

3.    Differences in Business Practices

Be more effective interacting with foreign clients and colleagues by understanding the patterns of fundamental business practices. What is acceptable behavior in one culture may not be acceptable in another.

Market research, reading books on countries or regions of the world, talking with a country specific consultant, and/or using the Internet to gain an understanding of correct multi-national business practices can hone these skills for a tradeshow. Try to understand the following:

*   First-meeting standards

*   Addressing a visitor properly

*   Careful wording of greetings

*   Offering hand shakes or other forms of recognition

*   Making eye contact

*   Watching body posture

*   Sensitivity to spatial distance

*   Initiating the conversation and asking questions

*   Appropriate manners and taboos

*   Establishing trust and sincerity

- Using appropriate metaphors
- Negotiating the sale or contract
- Determining who has authority and who negotiates for the company
- Defining who addresses price, quantity and quality issues
- Recognizing important procedures
- Knowing what details of the sale or contract are appropriate
- Setting appointments
- Importance of punctuality and promptness
- Establishing timeframes for decisions
- Garnering commitments
- Recognizing the ceremonial nature of business meetings
- Attitudes toward money, binding contracts, commitments, achievement and work
- Age and gender differences and how the differences are treated in business

## Post-show Follow Up with the International Buyer

Once the show is over and follow-up contact is in place, put the strategic business and marketing plan into action. These distinguish the company from the competition and establish a positive image.

- Send a letter to each buyer contacted before and during the show. An immediate response is important in establishing the relationship – much more so than in western cultures.

- Be sensitive to social, cultural, business and time differences when communicating. Soften the curt business language typical of western correspondence.

- Letters are more formal. Indicate a desire to open a working relationship in initial follow-up correspondence. Don't try a "hard sell" unless a specific sale has been agreed upon. Provide additional promotional material.

- Keep the points logical and relatively conventional. However, open the correspondence with a polite and complimentary statement.

- Clear wording and special attention to details prevent misunderstandings in language and business practices.

- Do not use jargon or phrases that may be unfamiliar in the buyer's culture.

- Make sure correspondence, return addresses and business cards include the country of origin, e.g., U.S.A., Canada, Brazil.

- Include fax numbers and e-mail addresses.

- International date follows a day/month/year format, e.g., 09 October 1998 or 09.10.98.

- Whenever possible, use titles, including yours and the foreign buyer's.

Clarify any inquiry or order and then develop a transaction-by-transaction quote. Return it quickly via fax. If developing this quote takes more than two days, contact the buyer and tell him when it will arrive. A good procedure for developing these quotes and eventually the proforma invoice are in the *Export Expert: The Complete Guide to the Global Trade Process*.

Pay attention to details of the international trade. Get help from export counselors, freight forwarders, international attorneys and accountants, or shipping lines if you have any questions.

Management of a foreign account may be handled differently. For example, a foreign company may require a less-democratic approach to decision making. Many companies are managed in an authoritarian fashion and are not as participatory as in Western cultures. Developing a long-term relationship prevents overstepping bounds and failed expectations.

## Evolve into a Global Expert – with an Attitude

Usually, entering the export marketplace is an extremely exciting venture and one most companies are glad they made the transition. The best way to become a global expert is to understand the international trade process and follow a few simple rules:

- Adapt an open-business style and social behavior that welcomes new and different audiences. Be sensitive to all cultures.

- Be non-judgmental. Try to adopt the attitude that the world is one big opportunity and flexibility and understanding are the keys to success.

- Learn what works, then find out why and make accommodations to strengthen the international position.

- Recognize that not everything is going to go as planned. Adjustments need to be made, and annoyances and irritations do not have to be deal-busters.

Mostly, keep a sense of humor about these new markets and realize that learning to grow and change is energizing for you, the company and the newly found foreign client.

Good Luck Going Global!

# Marcia A. Smith

Marcia A. Smith is founder and President of Columbia Cascade, Incorporated, a Reston, Virginia woman-owned small business founded in April 1984. Columbia Cascade specializes in software development in the field of artificial intelligence computer software systems.

Several years ago, Columbia Cascade recognized the need for a how-to-export system that would help companies enter and successfully compete in foreign markets. As a result, the company developed the *Export Expert: The Complete Guide to the Global Trade Process*, the first and only how-to-export software product available of its kind. The system is currently being used by new-to-export companies nationwide to evaluate their export potential and help them handle the entire export process. It is also being used extensively by existing exporting companies as a way of validating their current export strategy and as a means of training their staff and management on the export process. The system is endorsed by all the major U.S. government agencies involved in trade, including the Departments of Commerce and Agriculture, the Small Business Administration (SBA), Export-Import Bank, and Agency for International Development, plus most state development offices nationwide. The SBA, for example, has installed the system in every one of their Business Information Centers around the nation. *Export Expert* was chosen by the U.S. Chamber of Commerce and IBM to be included in their 1998 Technology Catalog for Small and Mid-sized Businesses. The *Export Expert* has been deemed the best how-to-export training tool by training and professional development practitioners and many educational institutions are using the software to teach international trade to business students.

Ms. Smith conducted the original research and development on the *Export Expert* and has been instrumental in bringing it to market and the export community at large. In addition to her active role providing export seminars, Ms. Smith is working with the publisher Addison Wesley Longman to combine the software system with one of the world's leading textbooks on international marketing and export management. She is also writing an international trade certification program that will be offered on the Internet. She is on the Board of Directors of the Small Business Exporters Association, a Director for the Center for International Business at Shenandoah University in Virginia, and serves on many national and international business development committees. Ms. Smith received the Small Business Exporters Association Outstanding Service Award in May 1997. She is a member of the National Association of Small Business International Trade Educators, the International Network for Women in Enterprise and Trade and the American Women's Business Consortium in Europe. Ms. Smith is an 11th generation American entrepreneur and speaks and trains nationally on the international trade process and exporting.

**EXPORT EXPERT**

*Opening Global Opportunities*

Columbia Cascade, Incorporated
12147 Stirrup Road, Suite 110
Reston, VA 20191-2103 U.S.A.
Tel: 703-860-0866 • Fax: 703-860-8449
Email: colcas@pipeline.com
www.columbiacascade.com